Level 2

¡Avancemos!

Unit 5 Resource Book

McDougal Littell
A DIVISION OF HOUGHTON MIFFLIN COMPANY
Evanston, Illinois • Boston • Dallas

Fine Art Acknowledgments

Page 86 *Still Life* (ca. 1925), Àngel Planells i Cruanyes. Oil on canvas. Collection J.B. Cendros, Barcelona. The Bridgeman Art Library.

Page 87 *Autumn*, or *The Grape Harvest* (1786-87), Francisco José de Goya y Lucientes. Oil on canvas. Prado, Madrid, Spain. Giraudon/The Bridgeman Art Library.

Page 87 *The Third of May, 1808* (1814), Francisco de Goya y Lucientes. 266 cm x 345 cm, oil on canvas. Erich Lessing/Art Resource, NY.

Page 88 *L'enfant aux pâtisseries* (*Child with Cakes*) (1921), María Blanchard. Oil on canvas. Musée National d'Art Moderne, Centre Pompidou, Paris/The Bridgeman Art Library.

Page 89 *Philip II of Spain* (1565), Sofonisba Anguisciola. Oil on canvas. Prado, Madrid, Spain/The Bridgeman Art Library.

ISBN-13: 978-0-618-75359-8
ISBN-10: 0-618-75359-1

2 3 4 5 6 7 8 9 - MDO- 12 11 10 09 08 07

McDougal Littell

¡Avancemos!

Table of Contents

To the Teacher

Welcome to *¡Avancemos!* This exciting new Spanish program from McDougal Littell has been designed to provide you—the teacher of today's foreign language classroom—with comprehensive pedagogical support.

PRACTICE WITH A PURPOSE

Activities throughout the program begin by establishing clear goals. Look for the **¡Avanza!** arrow that uses student-friendly language to lead the way towards achievable goals. Built-in self-checks in the student text (**Para y piensa:** Did you get it?) offer the chance to assess student progress throughout the lesson. Both the student text and the workbooks offer abundant leveled practice to match varied student needs.

CULTURE AS A CORNERSTONE

¡Avancemos! celebrates the cultural diversity of the Spanish-speaking world by motivating students to think about similarities and contrasts among different Spanish-speaking cultures. Essential questions encourage thoughtful discussion and comparison between different cultures.

LANGUAGE LEARNING THAT LASTS

The program presents topics in manageable chunks that students will be able to retain and recall. "Recycle" topics are presented frequently so students don't forget material from previous lessons. Previously learned content is built upon and reinforced across the different levels of the program.

TIME-SAVING TEACHER TOOLS

Simplify your planning with McDougal Littell's exclusive teacher resources: the all-inclusive EasyPlanner DVD-ROM, ready-made Power Presentations, and the McDougal Littell Assessment System.

Unit Resource Book

Each Unit Resource Book supports a unit of *¡Avancemos!* The Unit Resource Books provide a wide variety of materials to support, practice, and expand on the material in the *¡Avancemos!* student text.

Components **Following is a list of components included in each Unit Resource Book:**

BACK TO SCHOOL RESOURCES (UNIT 1 ONLY)

Review and start-up activities to support the **Lección preliminar** of the textbook.

DID YOU GET IT? RETEACHING & PRACTICE COPYMASTERS

If students' performance on the **Para y piensa** self-check for a section does not meet your expectations, consider assigning the corresponding Did You Get It? Reteaching and Practice Copymasters. These copymasters provide extensive reteaching and additional practice for every vocabulary and grammar presentation section in *¡Avancemos!* Each vocabulary and grammar section has a corresponding three-page copymaster. The first page of the copymaster reteaches the subject material in a fresh manner. Immediately following this presentation page are two pages of practice exercises that help the student master the topic. The practice pages have engaging contexts and structures to retain students' attention.

PRACTICE GAMES

These games provide fun practice of the vocabulary and grammar just taught. They are targeted in scope so that each game practices a specific area of the **lesson**: *Práctica de vocabulario*, *Vocabulario en contexto*, *Práctica de gramática*, *Gramática en contexto*, *Todo junto*, *Repaso de la lección*, and the lesson's cultural information.

Video and audio resources

VIDEO ACTIVITIES

These two-page copymasters accompany the Vocabulary Video and each scene of the **Telehistoria** in Levels 1 and 2 and the **Gran desafío** in Level 3. The pre-viewing activity asks students to activate prior knowledge about a theme or subject related to the scene they will watch. The viewing activity is a simple activity for students to complete as they watch the video. The post-viewing activity gives students the opportunity to demonstrate comprehension of the video episode.

VIDEO SCRIPTS

This section provides the scripts of each video feature in the unit.

AUDIO SCRIPTS

This section contains scripts for all presentations and activities that have accompanying audio in the student text as well as in the two workbooks (*Cuaderno: práctica por niveles* and *Cuaderno para hispanohablantes*) and the assessment program.

Culture resources

MAP/CULTURE ACTIVITIES

This section contains a copymaster with geography and culture activities based on the Unit Opener in the textbook.

FINE ART ACTIVITIES

The fine art activities in every lesson ask students to analyze pieces of art that have been selected as representative of the unit location country. These copymasters can be used in conjunction with the full-color fine art transparencies in the Unit Transparency Book.

Home-school connection

FAMILY LETTERS & FAMILY INVOLVEMENT ACTIVITIES

This section is designed to help increase family support of the students' study of Spanish. The family letter keeps families abreast of the class's progress, while the family involvement activities let students share their Spanish language skills with their families in the context of a game or fun activity.

ABSENT STUDENT COPYMASTERS

The Absent Student Copymasters enable students who miss part of a **lesson** to go over the material on their own. The checkbox format allows teachers to choose and indicate exactly what material the student should complete. The Absent Student Copymasters also offer strategies and techniques to help students understand new or challenging information.

Core Ancillaries in the ¡Avancemos! Program

Leveled workbooks

CUADERNO: PRÁCTICA POR NIVELES

This core ancillary is a leveled practice workbook to supplement the student text. It is designed for use in the classroom or as homework. Students who can complete the activities correctly should be able to pass the quizzes and tests. Practice is organized into three levels of difficulty, labeled A, B, and C. Level B activities are designed to practice vocabulary, grammar, and other core concepts at a level appropriate to most of your students. Students who require more structure can complete Level A activities, while students needing more of a challenge should be encouraged to complete the activities in Level C. Each level provides a different degree of linguistic support, yet requires students to know and handle the same vocabulary and grammar content.

The following sections are included in *Cuaderno: práctica por niveles* for each **lesson**:

- Vocabulario A, B, C
- Gramática 1 A, B, C
- Gramática 2 A, B, C
- Integración: Hablar
- Integración: Escribir
- Escuchar A, B, C
- Leer A, B, C
- Escribir A, B, C
- Cultura A, B, C

CUADERNO PARA HISPANOHABLANTES

This core ancillary provides leveled practice for heritage learners of Spanish. Level A is for heritage learners who hear Spanish at home but who may speak little Spanish themselves. Level B is for those who speak some Spanish but don't read or write it yet and who may lack formal education in Spanish. Level C is for heritage learners who have had some formal schooling in Spanish. These learners can read and speak Spanish, but may need further development of their writing skills. The *Cuaderno para hispanohablantes* will ensure that heritage learners practice the same basic grammar, reading, and writing skills taught in the student text. At the same time, it offers additional instruction and challenging practice designed specifically for students with prior knowledge of Spanish.

The following sections are included in *Cuaderno para hispanohablantes* for each **lesson**:

- Vocabulario A, B, C
- Vocabulario adicional
- Gramática 1 A, B, C
- Gramática 2 A, B, C
- Gramática adicional
- Integración: Hablar
- Integración: Escribir
- Lectura A, B, C
- Escritura A, B, C
- Cultura A, B, C

Other Ancillaries

ASSESSMENT PROGRAM

For each level of *¡Avancemos!*, there are four complete assessment options. Every option assesses students' ability to use the lesson and unit vocabulary and grammar, as well as assessing reading, writing, listening, speaking, and cultural knowledge. The on-level tests are designed to assess the language skills of most of your students. Modified tests provide more support, explanation and scaffolding to enable students with learning difficulties to produce language at the same level as their peers. Pre-AP* tests build the test-taking skills essential to success on Advanced Placement tests. The assessments for heritage learners are all in Spanish, and take into account the strengths that native speakers bring to language learning.

In addition to leveled lesson and unit tests, there is a complete array of vocabulary, culture, and grammar quizzes. All tests include scoring rubrics and point teachers to specific resources for remediation.

UNIT TRANSPARENCY BOOKS—1 PER UNIT

Each transparency book includes:

- Map Atlas Transparencies (Unit 1 only)
- Unit Opener Map Transparencies
- Fine Art Transparencies
- Vocabulary Transparencies
- Grammar Presentation Transparencies
- Situational Transparencies with Label Overlay (plus student copymasters)
- Warm Up Transparencies
- Student Book and Workbook Answer Transparencies

LECTURAS PARA TODOS

A workbook-style reader, *Lecturas para todos*, offers all the readings from the student text as well as additional literary readings in an interactive format. In addition to the readings, they contain reading strategies, comprehension questions, and tools for developing vocabulary.

There are four sections in each *Lecturas para todos*:

- *¡Avancemos!* readings with annotated skill-building support
- *Literatura adicional*—additional literary readings
- Academic and Informational Reading Development
- Test Preparation Strategies

* AP and the Advanced Placement Program are registered trademarks of the College Entrance Examination Board, which was not involved in the production of and does not endorse this product.

LECTURAS PARA HISPANOHABLANTES

Lecturas para hispanohablantes offers additional cultural readings for heritage learners and a rich selection of literary readings. All readings supported by reading strategies, comprehension questions, tools for developing vocabulary, plus tools for literary analysis.

There are four sections in each *Lecturas para hispanohablantes*:

- *En voces* cultural readings with annotated skill-building support
- *Literatura adicional*—high-interest readings by prominent authors from around the Spanish-speaking world. Selections were chosen carefully to reflect the diversity of experiences Spanish-speakers bring to the classroom.
- Bilingual Academic and Informational Reading Development
- Bilingual Test Preparation Strategies, for success on standardized tests in English

COMIC BOOKS

These fun, motivating comic books are written in a contemporary, youthful style with full-color illustrations. Each comic uses the target language students are learning. There is one 32-page comic book for each level of the program.

TPRS: TEACHING PROFICIENCY THROUGH READING AND STORYTELLING

This book includes an up-to-date guide to TPRS and TPRS stories written by Piedad Gutiérrez that use *¡Avancemos!* lesson-specific vocabulary.

MIDDLE SCHOOL RESOURCE BOOK

- Practice activities to support the 1b Bridge lesson
- Diagnostic and Bridge Unit Tests
- Transparencies
  - Vocabulary Transparencies
  - Grammar Transparencies
  - Answer Transparencies for the Student Text
  - Bridge Warm Up Transparencies
- Audio CDs

LESSON PLANS

- Lesson Plans with suggestions for modifying instruction
- Core and Expansion options clearly noted
- IEP suggested modifications
- Substitute teacher lesson plans

BEST PRACTICES TOOLKIT

Strategies for Effective Teaching

- Research-based Learning Strategies
- Language Learning that Lasts: Teaching for Long-term Retention
- Culture as a Cornerstone/Cultural Comparisons
- English Grammar Connection
- Building Vocabulary
- Developing Reading Skills
- Differentiation
- Best Practices in Teaching Heritage Learners
- Assessment (including Portfolio Assessment, Reteaching and Remediation)
- Best Practices Swap Shop: Favorite Activities for Teaching Reading, Writing, Listening, Speaking
- Reading, Writing, Listening, and Speaking Strategies in the World Languages classroom
- ACTFL Professional Development Articles
- Thematic Teaching
- Best Practices in Middle School

Using Technology in the World Languages Classroom

Tools for Motivation

- Games in the World Languages Classroom
- Teaching Proficiency through Reading and Storytelling
- Using Comic Books for Motivation

Pre-AP and International Baccalaureate

- International Baccalaureate
- Pre-AP

Graphic Organizer Transparencies

- Teaching for Long-term Retention
- Teaching Culture
- Building vocabulary
- Developing Reading Skills

Absent Student Copymasters—Tips for Students

LISTENING TO CDS AT HOME

- Open your text, workbook, or class notes to the corresponding pages that relate to the audio you will listen to. Read the assignment directions if there are any. Do these steps before listening to the audio selections.
- Listen to the CD in a quiet place. Play the CD loudly enough so that you can hear everything clearly. Keep focused. Play a section several times until you understand it. Listen carefully. Repeat aloud with the CD. Try to sound like the people on the CD. Stop the CD when you need to do so.
- If you are lost, stop the CD. Replay it and look at your notes. Take a break if you are not focusing. Return and continue after a break. Work in short periods of time: 5 or 10 minutes at a time so that you remain focused and energized.

QUESTION/ANSWER SELECTIONS

- If there is a question/answer selection, read the question aloud several times. Write down the question. Highlight the key words, verb endings, and any new words. Look up new words and write their meaning. Then say everything aloud.
- One useful strategy for figuring out questions is to put parentheses around groups of words that go together. For example: **(¿Cuántos niños)(van)(al estadio)(a las tres?)** Read each group of words one at a time. Check for meaning. Write out answers. Highlight key words and verb endings. Say the question aloud. Read the answer aloud. Ask yourself if you wrote what you meant.
- Be sure to say everything aloud several times before moving on to the next question. Check for spelling, verb endings, and accent marks.

FLASHCARDS FOR VOCABULARY

- If you have Internet access, go to ClassZone at classzone.com. All the vocabulary taught in *¡Avancemos!* is available on electronic flashcards. Look for the flashcards in the *¡Avancemos!* section of ClassZone.
- If you don't have Internet access, write the Spanish word or phrase on one side of a 3″ × 5″ card, and the English translation on the other side. Illustrate your flashcards when possible. Be sure to highlight any verb endings, accent marks, or other special spellings that will need a bit of extra attention.

GRAMMAR ACTIVITIES

- Underline or highlight all verb endings and adjective agreements. For example:
Nosotros comemos pollo rico.
- Underline or highlight infinitive endings: **trabajar**.
- Underline or highlight accented letters. Say aloud and be louder on the accented letters. Listen carefully for the loudness. This will remind you where to write your accent mark. For example: **lápiz**, **lápices**, **árbol**, **árboles**
- When writing a sentence, be sure to ask yourself, "What do I mean? What am I trying to say?" Then check your sentence to be sure that you wrote what you wanted to say.
- Mark patterns with a highlighter. For example, for stem-changing verbs, you can draw a "boot" around the letters that change:

v**ue**lvo	volvemos
v**ue**lves	volvéis
v**ue**lve	v**ue**lven

READING AND CULTURE SECTIONS

- Read the strategy box. Copy the graphic organizer so you can fill it out as you read.
- Look at the title and subtitles before you begin to read. Then look at and study any photos and read the captions. Translate the captions only if you can't understand them at all. Before you begin to read, guess what the selection will be about. What do you think that you will learn? What do you already know about this topic?
- Read any comprehension questions before beginning to read the paragraphs. This will help you focus on the upcoming reading selection. Copy the questions and highlight key words.
- Reread one or two of the questions and then go to the text. Begin to read the selection carefully. Read it again. On a sticky note, write down the appropriate question number next to where the answer lies in the text. This will help you keep track of what the questions have asked you and will help you focus when you go back to reread it later, perhaps in preparation for a quiz or test.
- Highlight any new words. Make a list or flashcards of new words. Look up their meanings. Study them. Quiz yourself or have a partner quiz you. Then go back to the comprehension questions and check your answers from memory. Look back at the text if you need to verify your answers.

PAIRED PRACTICE EXERCISES

- If there is an exercise for partners, practice both parts at home.
- If no partner is available, write out both scripts and practice both roles aloud. Highlight and underline key words, verb endings, and accent marks.

WRITING PROJECTS

- Brainstorm ideas before writing.
- Make lists of your ideas.
- Put numbers next to the ideas to determine the order in which you want to write about them.
- Group your ideas into paragraphs.
- Skip lines in your rough draft.
- Have a partner read your work and give you feedback on the meaning and language structure.
- Set it aside and reread it at least once before doing a final draft. Double-check verb endings, adjective agreements, and accents.
- Read it once again to check that you said what you meant to say.
- Be sure to have a title and any necessary illustrations or bibliography.

Did You Get It? *Presentación de vocabulario*

Level 2 pp. 254–255

¡AVANZA! **Goal:** Learn the terms to discuss foods, their flavors, and how to prepare them.

Foods, flavors, and preparation

- Many people follow a recipe (**una receta**) when they cook. Below is a list of foods and other ingredients (**ingredientes**) you can buy in almost any supermaket (**supermercado**).

Condiments
la sal *(salt)*
la pimienta *(pepper)*
la mayonesa *(mayonnaise)*
el ajo *(garlic)*
el aceite *(oil)*
el limón *(lemon)*
el vinagre *(vinegar)*
la mostaza *(mustard)*
el azúcar *(sugar)*

Foods
las espinacas *(spinach)*
la cebolla *(onion)*
la lechuga *(lettuce)*
la zanahoria *(carrot)*
la fresa *(strawberry)*

- Study these words that you can use to describe the flavor (**el sabor**) of the dishes you prepare.

agrio *(sour)*
salado *(salty)*
caliente *(hot)*
dulce *(sweet)*
picante *(spicy)*
delicioso *(delicious)*

- A popular dish in Spain is potato omelette (**la tortilla de patatas**). There are many ways to prepare it, but what is most important is that the ingredients are fresh (**frescos**). Here are some verbs you can use to talk about preparing foods.

freír *(to fry)*
cocinar *(to cook)*
mezclar *(to stir)*
hervir *(to boil)*
probar *(to taste)*
batir *(to beat)*
añadir *(to add)*

Nombre ______________________ Clase ______________ Fecha ______________

Did You Get It? *Práctica de vocabulario*

***Level 2* p. 256**

¡AVANZA! **Goal:** Learn the terms to discuss foods, their flavors, and how to prepare them.

❶ Match the following pictures with their Spanish terms.

a.

b.

c.

d.

e.

f.

g.

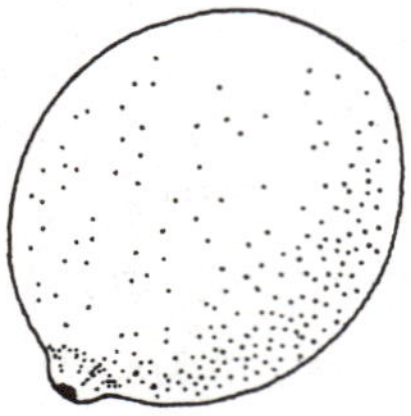
h.

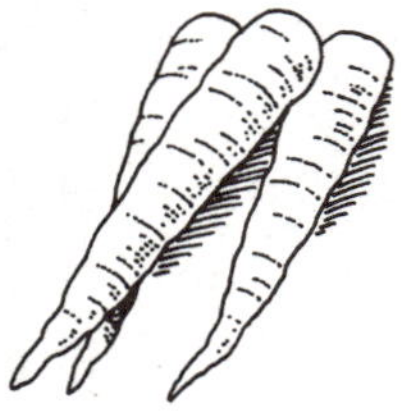
i.

1. _____ las espinacas
2. _____ el limón
3. _____ los huevos
4. _____ la cebolla
5. _____ las zanahorias
6. _____ las fresas
7. _____ el ajo
8. _____ la mayonesa
9. _____ la lechuga

❷ Complete the chart below to indicate when you use the ingredients in the box below. Some can be placed in more than one column.

el aceite	**el ajo**	**el azúcar**	**el limón**	**las espinacas**
la cebolla	**la lechuga**	**la mostaza**	**la pimienta**	**las fresas**
la mayonesa	**la sal**		**el vinagre**	**las zanahorias**

Algunos ingredientes para...		
El sándwich	**La cena**	**El postre**

Nombre ______________________ Clase ______________ Fecha ______________

3 Write which foods from the box below are being described.

el ajo	el azúcar	las fresas	las zanahorias	la mostaza	la tortilla de patatas

1. Es de sabor dulce. ______________________
2. Son frutas. ______________________
3. Es una comida típica española. ______________________
4. Es rica en sándwiches. ______________________
5. Son de color naranja. ______________________
6. Tiene sabor agrio. ______________________

4 Put the steps in this recipe in order by numbering them from 1 to 5.

____ Freír las patatas con la cebolla.
____ Mientras cocinan las patatas, batir los huevos.
____ Calentar el aceite.
____ Mezclar y freír los huevos con las patatas y la cebolla.
____ Comprar los ingredientes.

5 Answer in complete sentences the following questions about the foods you like to eat.

1. ¿Qué te gusta más, una tortilla de patatas o unos huevos fritos?
____
2. ¿Qué ingredientes necesitas para preparar una tortilla de patatas?
____
3. ¿Cuál es tu comida favorita?
____
4. ¿Comes las hamburguesas con mostaza o con mayonesa?
____
5. ¿Te gusta más comer los sándwiches con papas fritas o con espinacas?
____
6. ¿Prefieres las fresas con o sin azúcar?
____

Did You Get It? *Presentación de gramática*

Level 2 p. 259

¡AVANZA! **Goal:** Learn how to make **usted** and **ustedes** commands.

Regular *usted / ustedes* commands

- Read the sentences, paying attention to the boldfaced commands.

Singular	Plural	Meaning
Pruebe la tortilla.	**Prueben** la tortilla.	***Try*** *the tortilla.*
Añada un poco de sal.	**Añadan** un poco de sal.	***Add*** *a little salt.*
¡**Coma** la tortilla!	¡**Coman** la tortilla!	***Eat*** *the tortilla!*

EXPLANATION: Use the **yo** form of the present tense to form the **usted** command in Spanish. Drop the **-o** ending. Add **-e** to **-ar** verbs, and **-a** to **-er** and **-ir** verbs. Add **-n** to make the command plural. To make the command negative, simply place **no** in front of the verb.

Irregular *usted / ustedes* commands

- Now read these sentences, paying attention to the boldfaced commands.

Singular	Plural	Meaning
Dé un paseo.	**Den** un paseo.	***Take*** *a walk.*
Esté callado.	**Estén** callados.	***Be*** *quiet.*
Vaya a casa.	**Vayan** a casa.	***Go*** *home.*
Sepa la lección.	**Sepan** la lección.	***Know*** *the lesson.*
Sea bueno.	**Sean** buenos.	***Be*** *good.*

EXPLANATION: If the **yo** form of the verb in the present tense does not end with **-o**, this means the verb is irregular. These irregular forms need to be memorized.

Spelling changes

- Now study these boldfaced commands.

Singular	Plural	Meaning
Busque el libro.	**Busquen** el libro.	***Look*** *for the book.*
Pague el boleto.	**Paguen** el boleto.	***Pay*** *for the ticket.*
Empiece la lección.	**Empiecen** la lección.	***Begin*** *the lesson.*

EXPLANATION: The **-car**, **-gar**, and **-zar** verbs have the same spelling changes in the **usted / ustedes** commands as they do in the preterite tense.

Did You Get It? *Práctica de gramática*

Level 2 pp. 260–261

¡AVANZA! **Goal:** Learn how to make **usted** and **ustedes** commands.

1 Write the affirmative singular **usted** command for each verb.

1. buscar ______________
2. comprar ______________
3. batir ______________
4. hervir ______________
5. probar ______________
6. añadir ______________
7. comer ______________
8. empezar ______________
9. freír ______________
10. estudiar ______________

2 Write the negative singular **usted** command for each verb.

1. estar ______________
2. dar ______________
3. practicar ______________
4. ir ______________
5. desayunar ______________
6. poner ______________
7. mezclar ______________
8. ser ______________
9. freír ______________
10. leer ______________

3 Write the plural **ustedes** command for each verb.

1. no empezar ______________
2. entender ______________
3. no probar ______________
4. no ir ______________
5. almorzar ______________
6. no comer ______________
7. estar ______________
8. preparar ______________
9. no batir ______________
10. comprar ______________

❹ Answer each question using a singular **usted** command. Follow the model.

Modelo: ¿Compro patatas y cebollas?
Sí, compre patatas y cebollas.

1. ¿Bato los huevos?
____
2. ¿Corto las cebollas?
____
3. ¿Mezclo dos ajos con las cebollas y las patatas?
____
4. ¿Busco la mostaza?
____
5. ¿Empiezo a freír las patatas y las cebollas?
____
6. ¿Cocino todo durante quince minutos?
____

❺ Write one affirmative **usted / ustedes** command and one negative **usted / ustedes** command based on what you see in each picture.

Modelo:  *Compre las fresas. No compre las manzanas.*

1. añadir

2. freír / hervir

3. cocinar con

4. mezclar

1. _______________
2. _______________
3. _______________
4. _______________

Did You Get It? *Presentación de gramática*

Level 2 p. 264

¡AVANZA! **Goal:** Learn where to place pronouns with **usted** and **ustedes** commands.

Pronouns with commands

- **Affirmative commands**
  Study the following sentences, paying attention to the boldfaced words.

  Fría **las patatas.** *(Fry **the potatoes**.)* ⟶ Fría**las**. *(Fry **them**.)*
  Añada **las cebollas.** *(Add **the onions**.)* ⟶ Añáda**las**. *(Add **them**.)*
  Mezclen **los ingredientes.** *(Mix **the ingredients**.)* ⟶ Mézclen**los**. *(Mix **them**.)*
  Preparen **la ensalada.** *(Prepare **the salad**.)* ⟶ Prepáren**la**. *(Prepare **it**.)*

EXPLANATION: In affirmative commands, pronouns are *attached* to the command. If the pronoun is attached to an affirmative command that has more than two syllables, a written accent is placed over the third to the last syllable to keep the stress where it belongs.

- **Negative commands**
  Now study these sentences, paying attention to the boldfaced words.

  No fría **la hamburguesa.** *(Don't fry **the hamburger**.)* ⟶ No **la** fría. *(Don't fry **it**.)*
  No bata **el huevo.** *(Don't beat **the egg**.)* ⟶ No **lo** bata. *(Don't beat **it**.)*

EXPLANATION: In negative commands, pronouns are placed immediately *before* the command.

Did You Get It? *Práctica de gramática*

Level 2 pp. 265–266

¡AVANZA! **Goal:** Learn where to place pronouns with **usted** and **ustedes** commands.

1 Answer each question with an affirmative **usted** command, using a pronoun in place of the underlined noun. Follow the model.

Modelo: ¿Pongo el ajo en la cocina? *Sí, póngalo en la cocina.*

1. ¿Preparo la comida? ______________________
2. ¿Escribo un correo electrónico. ______________________
3. ¿Leo el libro? ______________________
4. ¿Escucho la música? ______________________
5. ¿Como las fresas? ______________________

2 Answer each question with a negative **usted** command, using a pronoun in place of the underlined noun. Follow the model.

Modelo: ¿Bato los huevos? *No, no los bata.*

1. ¿Cocino las zanahorias? ______________________
2. ¿Hiervo el aceite? ______________________
3. ¿Pruebo la receta? ______________________
4. ¿Mezclo la comida? ______________________
5. ¿Corto las cebollas? ______________________

3 Choose the correct command to complete each dialogue.

1. póngalas / las ponga

   —Carmen, ¿pongo las zanahorias en la sala?

   —No, no las necesito allí. ______________ en la cocina, por favor.

2. córtelos / los corte

   —¿Corto los ajos antes de mezclarlos con las patatas?

   —No, no ______________ . Póngalos enteros, por favor.

3. bátalos / los bata

   —¿Bato los huevos con las patatas?

   —Sí, ______________ , pero no los mezcle con las patatas.

4. prepárela / la prepare

   —¿Preparo la cena para los invitados?

   —No, no ______________ . Ponga la mesa.

Nombre ______________ Clase ______________ Fecha ______________

4 Rewrite each sentence using a pronoun in place of the underlined words. Follow the model.

Modelo: Compre la comida en el supermercado.
Cómprela en el supermercado.

1. Lea la receta antes de cocinar.
____
2. Busque los ingredientes.
____
3. Corte las cebollas.
____
4. No ponga la mayonesa en las cebollas.
____
5. Cocine las patatas antes de comerlas.
____
6. Añada la sal primero.
____
7. No toque el aceite cuando está caliente.
____
8. Pruebe la comida antes de servirla.
____

5 Translate the following pairs of sentences into Spanish, using the model as a guide.

Modelo: Put the carrots on the table. *Ponga las zanahorias en la mesa.*
Put them on the table. *Póngalas en la mesa.*

1. Cook the spinach. ______________
Cook it. ______________
2. Start the potato omelette. ______________
Start it now. ______________
3. Beat the eggs. ______________
Beat them. ______________
4. Fry the onions. ______________
Fry them. ______________
5. Add the salt. ______________
Add it. ______________
6. Mix the ingredients. ______________
Mix them. ______________

¿Recuerdas?

Level 2 p. 263

Staying healthy

- There are many things you can do to stay healthy. Study some of the ways below.

beber... *(to drink)*
agua *(water)*
jugo *(juice)*
leche *(milk)*
comer... *(to eat)*
verduras *(greens)*
zanahorias *(carrots)*
frutas *(fruits)*
espinacas *(spinach)*
ajo *(garlic)*
hacer ejercicio... *(to exercise)*
practicar deportes *(to play sports)*
correr *(to run)*
descansar *(to rest)*

Práctica

1 Complete the following chart telling people the top things you think they should do to stay healthy. One is written for you.

Para estar bien...

1. *Beban mucha agua.*
2. ______________________
3. ______________________
4. ______________________
5. ______________________
6. ______________________

Nombre ______________________ Clase ______________ Fecha ______________

¿Recuerdas?

Level 2 p. 265

Chores

- Study this list of chores in Spanish.

barrer el suelo	*(to sweep the floor)*
cortar el césped	*(to cut the grass)*
hacer la cama	*(to make the bed)*
lavar los platos	*(to wash the dishes)*
limpiar la cocina	*(to clean the kitchen)*
pasar la aspiradora	*(to vacuum)*
planchar la ropa	*(to iron)*
sacar la basura	*(to take out the trash)*

Práctica

Look at the pictures of Juan and Luisa's house. Tell them what they must do to clean it. The first one is done for you.

1.

2.

3.

4.

5.

6.

7.

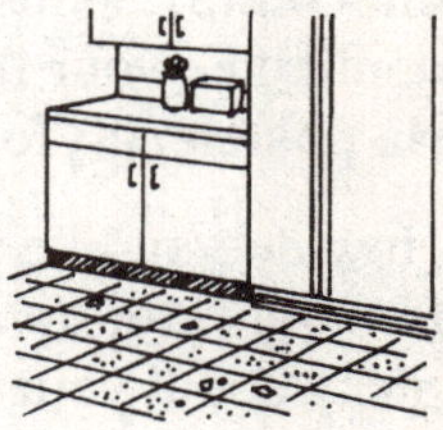
8.

1. *Hagan la cama. Háganla.*
2. ______________________
3. ______________________
4. ______________________
5. ______________________
6. ______________________
7. ______________________
8. ______________________

Did You Get It? *Presentación de vocabulario*

***Level 2* pp. 278–279**

¡AVANZA! **Goal:**	Learn to identify items in a place setting, describe various dishes, and order in a restaurant.

All about food

- **La mesa**

  You have invited a friend for dinner. First you set the table. Here's what you need.

  el plato *(plate)*
  el tenedor *(fork)*
  el cuchillo *(knife)*
  la cuchara *(spoon)*
  el vaso *(glass)*
  la servilleta *(napkin)*

- **La comida**

  Every good meal starts off with an appetizer (**un entremés**). If your friend prefers a vegetarian dish (**un plato vegetariano**), you could prepare spaghetti (**los espaguetis**) or cold vegetable soup (**un gazpacho**).

  If your friend likes meat, you might think about preparing grilled steak (**el filete a la parrilla**), pork chops (**unas chuletas de cerdo**), or roasted chicken (**un pollo asado**).

  If your friend enjoys seafood, consider a traditional Spanish rice dish prepared with any of a variety of items, such as prawns, mussels, shrimp, and sausage (**la paella**).

  For dessert, you could prepare custard (**el flan**) or a chocolate cake (**una tarta de chocolate**). Think about serving a cup of tea (**un té**) with dessert. Better yet, you could take your friend to the ice cream parlor (**la heladería**) or pastry shop (**la pastelería**) for sweets.

  How do you like your food prepared? Mixed (**mezclado/a**)? Beaten (**batido/a**)? Ground (**molido/a**)? Raw (**crudo/a**)? Cooked (**cocido/a**)? Fried (**frito/a**)? If you are picky about your food, make sure to ask for it the way you want it.

- **El restaurante**

  Maybe you don't want to cook at all! You might want to invite your friend to a restaurant where the waiters are very attentive (**muy atentos**) and the house specials (**las especialidades de la casa**) are appetizing. When the waiter asks what you want to eat (**para comer**), you can say *Could you bring...?* (**¿Me puede traer...?**)

Nombre ______________________ Clase ______________ Fecha ______________

Did You Get It? *Práctica de vocabulario*

Level 2 p. 280

¡AVANZA! **Goal:** Learn to identify items in a place setting, describe various dishes, and order in a restaurant.

1 Which would you use to eat or drink the following? For some foods you might use more than one item or utensil.

el tenedor	la cuchara	el cuchillo	el vaso

1. la sopa ______________________
2. la leche ______________________
3. los espaguetis ______________________
4. el helado ______________________
5. el filete ______________________
6. las espinacas ______________________
7. el té ______________________
8. las chuletas de cerdo ______________________
9. las papas hervidas ______________________

2 Write the name of the food shown in each picture.

1.

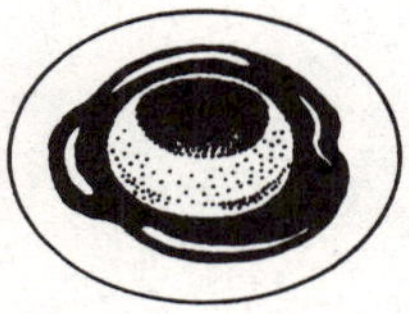
2.

3.

4.

5.

6.

7.

8.

1. ______________________ 5. ______________________
2. ______________________ 6. ______________________
3. ______________________ 7. ______________________
4. ______________________ 8. ______________________

Nombre ______________________ Clase ______________ Fecha ______________

3 Use the words and phrases in the box to complete the paragraph.

muy atenta	**los espaguetis**	**el entremés**	**el gazpacho**
el flan	**la tarta**	**verduras**	**especialidad de la casa**

Mi amigo Andrés y yo estamos en el Restaurante Madrid. La camarera es **1.** ______________________ y enseguida nos trae la carta. De entremés, pedimos **2.** ______________________ . Andrés es vegetariano. Él pide **3.** ______________________ . Una **4.** ______________________ es el filete a la parrilla. Yo no soy vegetariana. Pido el filete. También pido **5.** ______________________ cocidas. De postre, pido **6.** ______________________ y Andrés pide **7.** ______________________ de chocolate.

4 Imagine that you own a restaurant. Fill in the menu below with the house specials that you would offer.

ESPECIALIDADES DE LA CASA

Did You Get It? *Presentación de gramática*

¡AVANZA! **Goal:** Learn affirmative and negative words and how to use them correctly.

Affirmative and negative words

- Study the following sentences, paying attention to the boldfaced words.

No quiero **nada.** *(I **don't** want **anything**.* ⟶ Literal translation: *I do **not** want **nothing**.)*

No estudio **nunca.** *(I **don't** study **ever**.* ⟶ Literal translation: *I do **not** study **never**.)*

No hay **nadie.** *(There **isn't anyone**.* ⟶ Literal translation: *There is **not no one**.)*

EXPLANATION: Unlike English, Spanish not only allows you to use double negatives, it requires them! Study the pairs of affirmative and negative words below.

algo *(something)*	⟷	**nada** *(nothing)*
alguien *(someone)*	⟷	**nadie** *(nobody)*
algún / alguno(a) *(some)*	⟷	**ningún / ninguno(a)** *(none, not any)*
o... o *(either . . . or)*	⟷	**ni... ni** *(neither . . . nor)*
siempre *(always)*	⟷	**nunca** *(never)*
también *(also)*	⟷	**tampoco** *(neither, either)*

- Study the sentences, paying attention to the boldfaced words.

¿Conoces **a alguien** en ese restaurante? *(Do you know **anyone** at that restaurant?)*

No, no conozco **a nadie** ahí. *(No, I don't know **anyone** there.)*

EXPLANATION: Use **a** *before* **alguien** or **nadie** when they are *objects* of the verb.

- Study the dialogue, paying attention to the boldfaced words.

—¿Quieres **algún** postre? *(Do you want **any** dessert?)*

—No, no quiero **ningún** postre. *(No, I don't want **any** dessert.)*

EXPLANATION: Alguno(a) / ninguno(a) become **algún / ningún** *before* a masculine singular noun.

Did You Get It? *Práctica de gramática*

***Level 2* pp. 284–285**

¡AVANZA! **Goal:** Learn affirmative and negative words and how to use them correctly.

1 Match the opposites.

1. algo	ninguno
2. alguien	nada
3. también	ni... ni
4. alguno	tampoco
5. o... o	nadie

2 Rewrite the sentences to make them negative. Follow the model.

Modelo: Él pide o el pollo o la tortilla. ⟶ *No pide ni el pollo ni la tortilla.*

1. Sirve a alguien en el restaurante.

____

2. Saluda siempre a los clientes.

____

3. Prepara los postres también.

____

4. Busca alguna silla en el otro cuarto.

____

5. Pide o el flan o la tarta de chocolate.

____

3 Rewrite the sentences to make them affirmative. Follow the model.

Modelo: No sirvo a nadie. ⟶ *Sirvo a alguien.*

1. No pongo ningún vaso en la mesa.

____

2. No conozco a nadie en el restaurante.

____

3. No sirvo nunca los espaguetis.

____

4. No como ni el filete a la parrilla ni la paella.

____

5. No pido la tarta de chocolate tampoco.

____

❹ Choose words from the box to complete the dialogue.

algún	**algunas**	**ni... ni**	**ninguna**
también	**tampoco**	**ningún**	**o... o**

Adela: ¿Hay ______________ libro de cocina por aquí?

Sra. Martínez: No, Adela, no hay ______________ libro de cocina por aquí.

Adela: Bueno, podemos cocinar ______________ chuletas de cerdo hoy, ¿verdad?

Sra. Martínez: No, hoy no podemos preparar ______________ comida con carne porque viene mi hermano, que es vegetariano.

Adela: Ah, ¿sí? Estupendo. ¿Preparo las verduras crudas y el gazpacho?

Sra. Martínez: No, no prepare ______________ las verduras crudas ______________ el gazpacho.

Adela: ¿Preparo los espaguetis?

Sra. Martínez: No, ______________ prepare los espaguetis. Prepare ______________ las verduras cocidas ______________ el flan.

Adela: Muy bien. ¡Y ______________ preparo la tarta de chocolate!

❺ Answer **no** to everything. Follow the model.

Modelo: ¿Conoces a alguien ahí? *No, no conozco a nadie ahí.*

1. ¿Vas a comprar algo frío?
____

2. ¿Te gustan las verduras y el gazpacho?
____

3. ¿Conoces a alguien en la clase de cocina?
____

4. ¿Pides algo para beber?
____

5. En tu casa, ¿preparas siempre la comida?
____

6. ¿Quieres algún postre?
____

7. ¿Hay alguna comida sabrosa en la cafetería de la escuela?
____

Nombre ______________________ Clase ______________ Fecha ______________

Did You Get It? *Presentación de gramática*

***Level 2* p. 288**

¡AVANZA! **Goal:** Learn how to place two object pronouns in a sentence.

Double object pronouns

- Study the following sentences, paying attention to the boldfaced words, especially the two pronouns in the second sentence.

  El camarero **nos** sirve **el flan** a Beto y a mí.
  (The waiter serves ***the flan to Beto and me****.)*

  El camarero **nos lo** sirve.
  (The waiter serves ***it to us****.)*

EXPLANATION: When you have two object pronouns in the same sentence, the *indirect object pronoun* comes *first*.

- Study these sentences, paying attention to the boldfaced words, especially the two pronouns in the second sentence of each pair.

  Le doy **la propina** a la camarera. *(I give* ***the tip to the waitress****.)*
  Se la doy. *(I give* ***it to her****.)*

  Les vamos a traer **los filetes**. *(We are going to bring* ***you the steaks****.)*
  Se los vamos a traer. *(We are going to bring* ***them to you****.)*

EXPLANATION: When both the indirect and the direct object pronouns begin with *l*, the indirect object pronoun changes to **se**.

- Study these sentences, paying attention to the boldfaced words.

  Me la vas a traer. ⟶ Vas a **traérmela**. *(You're going to bring* ***it to me****.)*
  Se lo estoy pidiendo. ⟶ Estoy **pidiéndoselo**. *(I'm asking* ***him for it****.)*

EXPLANATION: When a conjugated verb appears with an *infinitive* or a verb in the **-ndo** form, the pronouns can go *before* the conjugated verb or *attached* to the infinitive or **-ndo** form. When pronouns are attached, a written *accent* is needed to keep the original stress.

Did You Get It? *Práctica de gramática*

Level 2 pp. 289–290

¡AVANZA! **Goal:** Learn how to place two object pronouns in a sentence.

1 Answer each question replacing the underlined noun with a pronoun. Follow the model.

Modelo: El camarero me trae el filete.
El camarero me lo trae.

1. El camarero les trae los espaguetis.
____
2. El camarero nos trae el plato vegetariano.
____
3. El camarero os trae el gazpacho.
____
4. El camarero te trae las chuletas de cerdo.
____
5. El camarero te trae la cuenta.
____

2 Rewrite the sentences, replacing the underlined nouns with pronouns. Follow the model.

Modelos: Voy a servir las chuletas a los clientes.
Voy a servírselas. *Se las voy a servir.*

Estoy poniendo los tenedores a los niños.
Estoy poniéndoselos. *Se los estoy poniendo.*

1. Voy a llevar el pollo asado al cliente.
______________________ ______________________
2. Estoy sirviendo el postre a los invitados.
______________________ ______________________
3. Voy a dar la cuenta al señor.
______________________ ______________________
4. Estoy preparando los entremeses para las señoras.
______________________ ______________________
5. Voy a traer la paella a los chicos.
______________________ ______________________

Nombre ______________ Clase ______________ Fecha ______________

3 Write two answers for each question. Follow the model.

Modelo: ¿A quién le vas a dar estas fresas con azúcar? *(a Ana)*
Voy a dárselas a Ana. *Se las voy a dar a Ana.*

1. ¿A quién le vas a dar este té con limón? *(a mi papá)*
____
____
2. ¿A quién le vas a llevar las chuletas? *(a la abuela)*
____
____
3. ¿A quién le vas a servir esta comida? *(a mis padres)*
____
____
4. ¿A quién le vas a llevar este flan? *(a Tomás)*
____
____
5. ¿A quién le vas a dar estos postres? *(a mis amigos)*
____
____
6. ¿A quién le vas a servir esta tarta de chocolate? *(a los invitados)*
____
____

4 Translate the following sentences into Spanish, replacing the underlined nouns with pronouns. Follow the model.

Modelo: The waiter brings the bill to the client.
El camarero se la trae al cliente.

1. The waiter serves the pork chops to the ladies.
____
2. The man asks the waiter for the bill.
____
3. I give the book to my friend.
____
4. He takes the fruit to Tomás.
____

¿Recuerdas?

Level 2 p. 282

Prepositions of location

- Study the following list of words.

en	*(on / in)*	**enfrente de**	*(across from / in front of)*
entre	*(between)*	**delante de**	*(in front of)*
al lado de	*(next to)*	**detrás de**	*(behind)*
alrededor de	*(around)*		
lejos de	*(far from)*	**encima de**	*(on top of)*
cerca de	*(near, close to)*	**debajo de**	*(under, underneath)*
		dentro de	*(inside of)*
a la izquierda de	*(to the left of)*		
a la derecha de	*(to the right of)*		

Práctica

State where the following objects and people are based on the picture. Follow the model.

Modelo:

el chico / la chica
El chico está al lado de la chica.

1. el tenedor / el plato
____

2. el cuchillo / el plato
____

3. el plato / la mesa
____

4. el plato / el cuchillo y el tenedor
____

5. el vaso / las fresas
____

Nombre ______________________ Clase ______________ Fecha ______________

¿Recuerdas?

Level 2 **p. 289**

Pronoun placement with commands

- Object pronouns are *attached* to the end of affirmative commands. They come *before* negative commands. Study these commands.

  Traiga la comida. *(Bring the food.)* ⟶ **Tráigala.** *(Bring it.)*
  No traiga la comida. *(Don't bring the food.)* ⟶ **No la traiga.** *(Don't bring it.)*

- To keep the original stress, a written *accent* is needed on commands that have pronouns attached. For example:

  Deme la receta. *(Give me the recipe.)* ⟶ **Démela.** *(Give it to me.)*

- When two pronouns start with *l*, the first pronoun changes to **se**. For example:

  Él lo trae a ella. ⟶ **Se** lo trae. *(He brings it **to her**.)*
  Él lo trae a él. ⟶ **Se** lo trae. *(He brings it **to him**.)*
  Él lo trae a ellos. ⟶ **Se** lo trae. *(He brings it **to them**.)*

  } Tráiga**se**lo. *(Bring it to him/her/them.)*

Práctica

Change each sentence to an affirmative and then negative command. Follow the model.

Modelo: El camarero me trae la cuenta.
Tráigamela.
No me la traiga.

1. El camarero nos sirve la comida.

____

____

2. La señora Gómez me prepara las chuletas.

____

____

3. Usted les da la receta.

____

____

4. Ustedes le traen el gazpacho.

____

____

Did You Get It? Answer Key

PRÁCTICA DE VOCABULARIO

FOODS, FLAVORS, AND PREPARATION, pp. 2–3

1

1. c
2. h
3. d
4. g
5. i
6. b
7. f
8. e
9. a

2 *Answers may vary.*

El sándwich: la pimienta, la sal, la mayonesa, la mostaza, el aceite, la lechuga

La cena: la pimienta, la sal, el ajo, el aceite, el limón, el vinagre, las espinacas, la cebolla, la lechuga, las zanahorias

El postre: el azúcar, las fresas, el limón

3

1. el azúcar
2. las fresas
3. la tortilla de patatas
4. la mostaza
5. las zanahorias
6. el ajo

4 *Answers may vary slightly.*

[3] Freír las patatas con la cebolla.

[4] Mientras cocinan las patatas, batir los huevos.

[2] Calentar el aceite.

[5] Mezclar y freír los huevos con las patatas y la cebolla.

[1] Comprar los ingredientes.

5 *Answers will vary.*

PRÁCTICA DE GRAMÁTICA

USTED / USTEDES COMMANDS, pp. 5–6

1

1. busque
2. compre
3. bata
4. hierva
5. pruebe
6. añada
7. coma
8. empiece
9. fría
10. estudie

2

1. no esté
2. no dé
3. no practique
4. no vaya
5. no desayune
6. no ponga
7. no mezcle
8. no sea
9. no fría
10. no lea

3

1. no empiecen
2. entiendan
3. no prueben
4. no vayan
5. almuercen
6. no coman
7. estén
8. preparen
9. no batan
10. compren

Did You Get It? Answer Key

4

1. Sí, bata los huevos.
2. Sí, corte las cebollas.
3. Sí, mezcle dos ajos con las cebollas y las patatas.
4. Sí, busque la mostaza.
5. Sí, empiece a freír las patatas y las cebollas.
6. Sí, cocine todo durante quince minutos.

5 *Answers may vary.*

1. Añadan sal. No añadan azúcar.
2. Fría la hamburguesa. No hierva la hamburguesa.
3. Cocine con aceite. No cocine con agua.
4. Mezcle las patatas con el ajo. No mezcle las patatas con la mostaza.

PRÁCTICA DE GRAMÁTICA

PRONOUNS WITH COMMANDS, pp. 8–9

1

1. Sí, prepárela.
2. Sí, escríbalo.
3. Sí, léalo.
4. Sí, escúchela.
5. Sí, cómalas.

Did You Get It? Answer Key

2

1. No, no las cocine.
2. No, no lo hierva.
3. No, no la pruebe.
4. No, no la mezcle.
5. No, no las corte.

3

1. Póngalas
2. los corte
3. bátalos
4. la prepare

4

1. Léala antes de cocinar.
2. Búsquelos.
3. Córtelas.
4. No la ponga en las cebollas.
5. Cocínelas antes de comerlas.
6. Añádala primero.
7. No lo toque cuando está caliente.
8. Pruébela antes de servirla.

5

1. Cocine las espinacas. Cocínelas.
2. Empiece la tortilla de patatas. Empiécela ahora.
3. Bata los huevos. Bátalos.
4. Fría las cebollas. Fríalas.
5. Añada la sal. Añádala.
6. Mezcle los ingredientes. Mézclelos.

¿RECUERDAS?

STAYING HEALTHY, p. 10

Práctica

Answers will vary.

¿RECUERDAS?

CHORES, p. 11

Práctica

1. *Hagan la cama. Háganla.*
2. Laven los platos. Lávenlos.
3. Corten el césped. / Córtenlo.
4. Planchen la ropa. Plánchenla.
5. Pasen la aspiradora. Pásenla.
6. Saquen la basura. Sáquenla.
7. Limpien la cocina. Límpienla.
8. Barran el suelo. Bárranlo.

Did You Get It? Answer Key

PRÁCTICA DE VOCABULARIO

ALL ABOUT FOOD, pp. 13–14

❶

1. la cuchara
2. el vaso
3. el tenedor / la cuchara / el cuchillo
4. la cuchara
5. el cuchillo / el tenedor
6. el tenedor
7. el vaso
8. el cuchillo / el tenedor
9. el tenedor

❷

1. el filete a la parrilla
2. el flan
3. las chuletas de cerdo
4. la tarta de chocolate
5. el pollo (asado)
6. la sopa
7. los espaguetis
8. la paella

❸

Mi amigo Andrés y yo estamos en el Restaurante Madrid. La camarera es **1. muy atenta** y enseguida nos trae la carta. De entremés, pedimos **2. el gazpacho**. Andrés es vegetariano. Él pide **3. los espaguetis**. Una **4. especialidad de la casa** es el filete a la parrilla. Yo no soy vegetariana. Pido el filete. También pido **5. verduras** cocidas. De postre, pido **6. el flan** y Andrés pide **7. la tarta** de chocolate.

❹ *Answers will vary.*

Did You Get It? Answer Key

PRÁCTICA DE GRAMÁTICA

AFFIRMATIVE AND NEGATIVE WORDS, pp. 16–17

❶

1. nada
2. nadie
3. tampoco
4. ninguno
5. ni... ni

❷

1. No sirve a nadie en el restaurante.
2. No saluda nunca a los clientes.
3. No prepara los postres tampoco.
4. No busca ninguna silla en el otro cuarto.
5. No pide ni el flan ni la tarta de chocolate.

❸

1. Pongo algún vaso en la mesa.
2. Conozco a alguien en el restaurante.
3. Sirvo siempre los espaguetis.
4. Como o el filete a la parilla o la paella.
5. Pido la tarta de chocolate también.

❹

Adela: ¿Hay **algún** libro de cocina por aquí?

Sra. Martínez: No, Adela, no hay **ningún** libro de cocina por aquí.

Adela: Bueno, podemos cocinar **algunas** chuletas de cerdo hoy, ¿verdad?

Sra. Martínez: No, hoy no podemos preparar **ninguna** comida con carne porque viene mi hermano, que es vegetariano.

Adela: Ah, ¿sí? Estupendo. ¿Preparo las verduras crudas y el gazpacho?

Sra. Martínez: No, no prepare **ni** las verduras crudas **ni** el gazpacho.

Adela: ¿Preparo los espaguetis?

Sra. Martínez: No, **tampoco** prepare los espaguetis. Prepare **o** las verduras cocidas **o** el flan.

Adela: Muy bien. ¡Y **también** preparo la tarta de chocolate!

❺

1. No, no voy a comprar nada frío.
2. No, no me gustan ni las verduras ni el gazpacho.
3. No, no conozco a nadie en la clase de cocina.
4. No, no pido nada para beber.
5. No, en mi casa no preparo nunca la comida.
6. No, no quiero ningún postre.
7. No, no hay ninguna comida sabrosa en la cafetería de la escuela.

Did You Get It? Answer Key

PRÁCTICA DE GRAMÁTICA

DOUBLE OBJECT PRONOUNS, pp. 19–20

1

1. El camarero se los trae.
2. El camarero nos lo trae.
3. El camarero os lo trae.
4. El camarero te las trae.
5. El camarero te la trae.

2

1. Voy a llevárselo. Se lo voy a llevar.
2. Estoy sirviéndoselo. Se lo estoy sirviendo.
3. Voy a dársela. Se la voy a dar.
4. Estoy preparándoselos. Se los estoy preparando.
5. Voy a traérsela. Se la voy a traer.

3

1. Voy a dárselo a mi papá. Se lo voy a dar a mi papá.
2. Voy a llevárselas a la abuela. Se las voy a llevar a la abuela.
3. Voy a servírsela a mis padres. Se la voy a servir a mis padres.
4. Voy a llevárselo a Tomás. Se lo voy a llevar a Tomás.
5. Voy a dárselos a mis amigos. Se los voy a dar a mis amigos.
6. Voy a servírsela a los invitados. Se la voy a servir a los invitados.

4

1. El camarero se las sirve a las señoras.
2. El hombre se la pide al camarero.
3. Se lo doy a mi amigo.
4. Se la lleva a Tomás.

¿RECUERDAS?

PREPOSITIONS OF LOCATION, p. 21

Práctica

1. El tenedor está a la izquierda del plato.
2. El cuchillo está a la derecha del plato.
3. El plato está encima de la mesa.
4. El plato está entre el cuchillo y el tenedor.
5. El vaso está lejos de las fresas.

¿RECUERDAS?

PRONOUN PLACEMENT WITH COMMANDS, p. 22

Práctica

1. Sírvanosla. No nos la sirva.
2. Prepáremelas. No me las prepare.
3. Désela. No se la dé.
4. Tráiganselo. No se lo traigan.

Adivinanzas *Práctica de vocabulario*

Solve the riddles by stating what dish is described.

1. Quiero cenar algo sabroso
pero yo soy muy perezoso.
Frío unas patatas con un huevo.
Este plato español no es nuevo.

¿Qué plato hace? ____________

2. Voy a cocinar
antes de ir a trabajar.
La lechuga es el gran ingrediente,
y no hay nada en ello caliente.

¿Qué hace? ____________

3. Voy a hacer un postre delicioso.
Manzanas, uvas y bananas. ¡Sabroso!
También pongo una fresa,
pero no pongo nada de mayonesa.

¿Qué hace? ____________

Nombre ______________________ Clase ______________ Fecha ______________

¿Qué palabra es? *Vocabulario en contexto*

Rearrange the letters in each vertical column to make a word from the **Vocabulario.** When you have found the scrambled word in each column, align each word in the box below in order to fill the middle row with a hidden word from the **Vocabulario.**

N	U	M	V	R	L	C	Í	H	E	U	L
S	D	P	R	O	N	R	R	A	E	D	L
A	E	A	I	O	Ó	E	R	L	C	E	O
A	C	T	R	A	I	L	F	C	T	R	I
P	L	I	H	S	M	Z	E	G	I	Y	T
C		I	E	S		M		U	A	A	T
S		N		B		A		E		N	A
I		E								S	R
E										A	

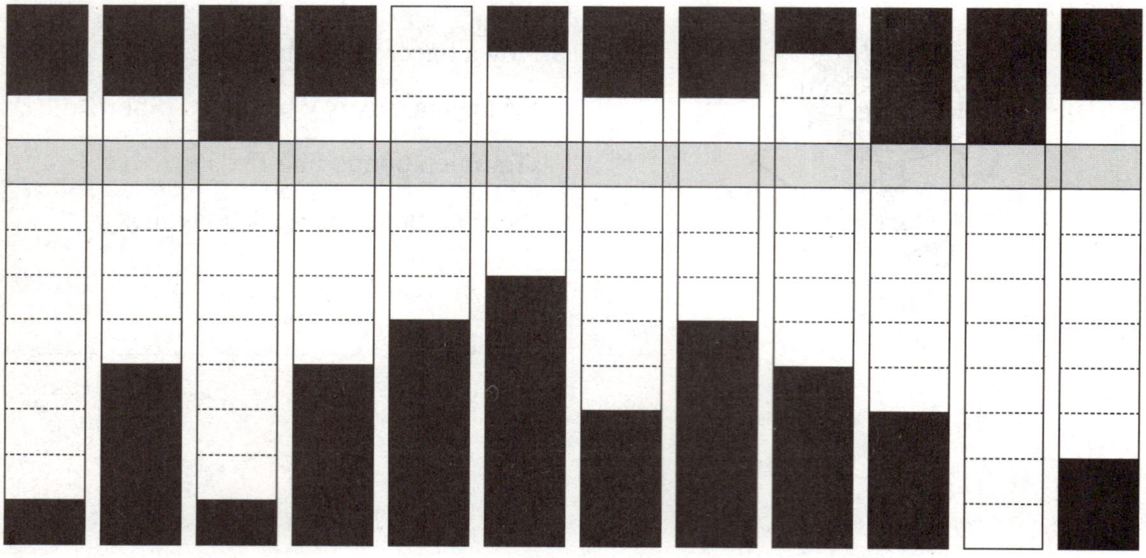

Nombre ______________________ Clase ______________ Fecha ______________

Letra perdida *Práctica de gramática*

Add one letter to each circled set of letters in order to form an **usted** command. Keep track of the letters that you have added in the space provided below. After you have collected all of the missing letters, rearrange them to form a nice addition to an **usted** command.

pnga

aya

ría

sea

puebe

pgue

cma

___ ___ R ___ ___ ___ ___ ___

UNIDAD 5 Lección 1

Practice Games

Nombre ______________________ Clase ______________ Fecha ______________

Crucigrama *Gramática en contexto*

Use the correct form of the **usted** or **ustedes** commands to complete the sentences and fill in the crossword puzzle.

Horizontal (*Across*)

2. Por favor, no ______________ usted malo con la maestra. (**ser**)

4. ______________ ustedes al hotel antes de las diez. (**regresar**)

5. ______________ usted en el mercado para sacar un buen precio. (**regatear**)

7. No ______________ ustedes al parque después de las ocho. (**ir**)

Abajo (*Down*)

1. ______________ ustedes la cuenta y yo pago la propina. (**pagar**)

3. No ______________ ustedes miedo de la montaña rusa. (**tener**)

6. ______________ usted ejercicio todos los días. (**hacer**)

Nombre ______________ Clase ______________ Fecha ______________

Busca la letra perdida *Práctica de gramática 2*

Add the correct **pronouns** and fill in the missing letters of the **usted** commands. Keep track of all the boxed letters that you have added in the space provided below. After you have collected all of the missing boxed letters, rearrange them to form an **usted** *command* and *pronoun* from the lesson. Number 1 is completed as an example.

1. No lo co [m] pre. (usted / azúcar)
2. No ___ ___ añad [ ]. (usted / sal)
3. Méz [ ] len ___ ___. (ustedes / ensalada)
4. No ___ ___ beb [ ] n. (ustedes / agua)
5. [ ] éa ___ ___. (usted / receta)
6. [ ] épa ___ ___ ___. (usted / ingredientes)
7. No ___ ___ ___ c [ ] rten. (ustedes / ajos)

¡ ___ ___ M ___ ___ ___ ___ !

(Hint: What you should do with vegetables.)

UNIDAD 5 Lección 1 Practice Games

Nombre ______________________ Clase ______________ Fecha ______________

Palabras con T y L *Todo junto*

Zelda and Carla are reading different recipes. Zelda's recipe only contains cooking words and ingredients with the letter **T**. Carla's recipe only contains words and ingredients with the letter **L** (don't count definite articles). Find all the words from **Vocabulario** that could be on each list.

Zelda "T"	Carla "L"
______________	______________
______________	______________
______________	______________
______________	______________
______________	______________
______________	______________
______________	______________
______________	______________

Which recipe has the most ingredients and words? ______________

UNIDAD 5 Lección 1

Practice Games

Nombre ______________________ Clase ______________ Fecha ______________

Ordena las letras *Lectura cultural*

Starting with the letter **P**, spell out the prize won by poet Pablo Neruda in 1971 by moving one space at a time horizontally, vertically, or diagonally. Do not reuse letters. Hint: watch out for distractors!

E	D	**P**	A	L	M	I
L	I	L	R	E	T	O
O	T	A	E	B	A	N
E	R	T	U	R	O	I

UNIDAD 5 Lección 1 Practice Games

Tienes... *Repaso de la lección*

Figure out the nine-letter word that describes **tortilla de patatas**. You'll find the nine letters by solving the sentence puzzles. Hint: circle all the letters that the two words from **Vocabulario** have in common, and then eliminate those that are also in the third word.

Es ____ ____ ____ ____ ____ ____ ____ ____ ____ .

1. This letter is in **mercado** and **ingredientes**, but not in **fresas**. ____
2. This letter is in **fresca** and **caliente**, but not in **azúcar**. ____
3. This letter is in **dulce** and **sal**, but not in **asco**. ____
4. This letter is in **limón** and **agrio**, but not in **sabroso**. ____
5. This letter is in **espinacas** and **cebolla**, but not in **huevo**. ____
6. This letter is in **batir** and **hervir**, but not in **cenar**. ____
7. This letter is in **probar** and **mostaza**, but not in **picante**. ____
8. This letter is in **sabor** and **mayonesa**, but not in **ajo**. ____
9. This letter is in **tortilla** and **pimienta**, but not in **ingrediente**. ____

Nombre ______________________ Clase ______________ Fecha ______________

¿Cuáles son las combinaciones? *Práctica de vocabulario*

Identify the following two-word combinations from **Vocabulario** using the parts of the combinations shown in each box.

___ [OL] ___ ___   ___ [SA] ___ ___

___ ___ [AT] ___   ___ ___ ___ ___ [TA] ___ ___ ___ ___ ___

¡ ___ [UE] ___   ___ ___ ___ [VE] ___ ___ ___ !

___ [UY]   ___ ___ [AB] ___ ___

Nombre ______________________ Clase ______________ Fecha ______________

¿Qué palabra es? *Vocabulario en contexto*

Rearrange the letters in each vertical column to make a word from **Vocabulario**. When you have found the scrambled word in each column, align each word in the box below in order fill the middle row with a hidden word from **Vocabulario**.

Z	A	D	T	E	F	M	R	O	O
O	L	S	D	T	N	T	T	I	T
C	E	A	A	R	A	R	T	M	D
P	A	A	R	R	L	S	A	D	B
G	L	O	N	A		E	A	L	I
H	P		E			E		A	A
A			E			N			
A						É			

UNIDAD 5 Lección 2
Practice Games

Nombre ______________________ Clase ______________ Fecha ______________

¿Qué hiciste? *Práctica de gramática 1*

Use the clues to fill in the missing letters of the affirmative or negative words to find out what these people did.

1. Elena y yo no comimos n ___ ___ a en la cafetería.
2. Guillermo atendió a a l ___ ___ i ___ ___ en el restaurante.
3. Trini me pidió ___ l ___ o pero no la oí.
4. Esteban y Eloisa ___ i e ___ ___ r ___ piden flan de postre.
5. Tú t ___ m ___ ___ é ___ vas al supermercado ¿verdad?
6. Vosotros t ___ m ___ ___ c___ tenéis tarea.
7. Eduardo no vio n ___ n ___ ___ n tenedor en la cocina.

UNIDAD 5 Lección 2 Practice Games

Letra perdida *Gramática en contexto*

Add one letter to each circled set of letters in order to form an affirmative or negative word. Keep track of the letters that you have added in the space provided below. After you have collected all of the missing letters, rearrange them to form an affirmative word from the lesson.

nad

unca

nade

ninuna

sempre

algna

ago

___ ___ ___ ___ ___ ___ ___

Nombre ____________________ Clase ____________ Fecha ____________

Busca la letra perdida *Práctica de gramática 2*

Fill in the blanks with the correct double object pronouns. Then arrange the letters in the boxes to discover a hidden word.

Anoche fui a comer con mi familia. Mi mamá quería una ensalada de espinacas entonces ella ___ ___ [___] [___] pidió al camarero. Mi hermana pidió el gazpacho y ___ [___] ___ ___ comió rapidito! A mi papá le gustan las chuletas entonces ___ ___ ___ [___] ___ pidió para él. Yo pedí un caldo de entremés pero el mesero ___ [___] ___ ___ trajo junto con la cena. Pedimos una paella para todos y el mesero ___ ___ ___ ___ [___] trajo primero. Al final pedimos dos flanes para compartir y ___ ___ ___ [___] ___ ___ comimos con el té.

Palabra escondida:

___ ___ H ___ ___ ___ D ___ R Í ___

Hint: a great place for dessert!

UNIDAD 5 Lección 2 Practice Games

Comida escondida *Todo junto*

(*Hidden foods*) There is a food hidden in each sentence. Can you find it? Hint: you will have to look in all the words in each item to find the answer.

1. Prefieren chuletas. ___ ___ ___ ___
2. Mezclan comidas. ___ ___ ___ ___ ___
3. Cenaron tarde. ___ ___ ___ ___ ___
4. Batiste fresas. ___ ___ ___ ___ ___
5. Probaron las chuletas. ___ ___ ___ ___ ___ ___
6. Es una sopa vegetariana. ___ ___ ___ ___ ___ ___ ___ ___ ___ ___
7. Fríen los ingredientes. ___ ___ ___ ___ ___ ___

Nombre ______________________ Clase ______________ Fecha ______________

Ordena las letras *Lectura cultural*

Starting with the letter **L**, spell out a traditional Uruguayan meat dish by moving one space at a time horizontally, vertically, or diagonally. Do not reuse letters. Hint: watch out for distractors!

A	R	A	L	D	E	D
R	P	I	A	M	E	I
A	L	D	O	O	V	A
L	I	N	T	E	P	L

Nombre ______________________ Clase ______________ Fecha ______________

¿Cómo te va? *Repaso de la lección*

Figure out the nine-letter word that states how we hope you're doing in Spanish class. You'll find the nine letters by solving the sentence puzzles. Hint: circle all the letters that the two words from **Vocabulario** have in common, and then eliminate those that are also in the third word.

Me va ___ ___ ___ ___ ___ ___ ___ ___ ___ .

1. This letter is in **atento** and **té**, but not in **tarta**. ___
2. This letter is in **excavación** and **examen**, but not in **pimienta**. ___
3. This letter is in **gazpacho** and **caldo**, but not in **tomate**. ___
4. This letter is in **paella** and **espaguetis**, but not in **parilla**. ___
5. This letter is in **flan** and **pollo**, but not in **tarta**. ___
6. This letter is in **mezclado** and **hervido**, but not in **batido**. ___
7. This letter is in **entremés** and **tenedor**, but not in **servilleta**. ___
8. This letter is in **plato** and **tarta**, but not in **vaso**. ___
9. This letter is in **cerdo** and **chocolate**, but not in **crudo**. ___

Practice Games Answer Key

PAGE 29

Práctica de vocabulario

1. la tortilla de patatas
2. una ensalada
3. una ensalada de frutas

PAGE 30

Vocabulario en contexto

				S							
				A	L			L			
E	D		H	B	I	M	F	E			T
S	U	P	E	R	M	E	R	C	A	D	O
P	L	I	R	O	Ó	Z	E	H	C	E	R
I	C	M	V	S	N	C	I	U	E	S	T
N	E	I	I	O		L	R	G	I	A	I
A		E	R			A		A	T	Y	L
C		N				R			E	U	L
A		T								N	A
S		A								A	
										R	

PAGE 31

Práctica de gramática 1

ponga, vaya, fría, sepa, pruebe, pague, coma; por favor

PAGE 32

Gramática en contexto

1. regresen
2. tengan
3. sea
4. paguen
5. regatee
6. haga
7. vayan

UNIDAD 5 Lección 1 Practice Games Answer Key

Practice Games Answer Key

PAGE 33

Práctica de gramática

1. lo, m
2. la, a
3. la, c
4. lo, a
5. la, L
6. los, S
7. los, o

Bonus: cómalas

PAGE 34

Todo junto

Which recipe has the most ingredients and words? Zelda

PAGE 35

Lectura cultural

Premio Nobel de Literatura

PAGE 36

Repaso de la lección

1. D
2. E
3. L
4. I
5. C
6. I
7. O
8. S
9. A

Es deliciosa.

Practice Games Answer Key

PAGE 37

Práctica de vocabulario

1. pollo asado
2. plato vegetariano
3. ¡Buen provecho!
4. Muy amable.

PAGE 38

Vocabulario en contexto

						E			
G				T		N		M	
A				R		T	T	O	
Z	P	A	A	A	F	R	A	L	B
P	A	S	T	E	L	E	R	I	A
A	E	A	E	R	A	M	T	D	T
C	L	D	N		N	É	A	A	I
H	L	O	D			S			D
O	A		E						O
			R						

PAGE 39

Práctica de gramática 1

1. nada
2. alguien
3. algo
4. siempre
5. también
6. tampoco
7. ningún

PAGE 40

Gramática en contexto

nad**a**, **n**unca, nadi**e**, nin**g**una, s**i**empre, alg**u**na, al**g**o; alguien

UNIDAD 5 Lección 2 Practice Games Answer Key

Practice Games Answer Key

PAGE 41

Práctica de gramática 2

se la, se lo, se las, me lo, nos la, nos los; palabra escondida: la heladería

PAGE 34

Todo junto

1. flan
2. caldo
3. cerdo
4. tarta
5. paella
6. espaguetis
7. filete

PAGE 43

Lectura cultural

La parrillada de Montevideo

PAGE 44

Repaso de la lección

1. E
2. X
3. C
4. E
5. L
6. E
7. N
8. T
9. E

Nombre _______________ Clase _______________ Fecha _______________

Video Activities *Vocabulario*

PRE-VIEWING ACTIVITY

Think about your favorite meal. Write five sentences describing that meal. What dishes are served? How are they prepared? How do they taste?

____

____

____

____

____

____

VIEWING ACTIVITY

Read the following events. While you watch the video indicate with a checkmark (✓) which of the events occurs in the video.

_______ **1.** Beatriz y José Luis preparan la cena.

_______ **2.** Beatriz hierve unas zanahorias.

_______ **3.** Beatriz fríe la mostaza y el vinagre.

_______ **4.** Beatriz bate los huevos y añade las espinacas.

_______ **5.** José Luis mira todas las recetas.

_______ **6.** José Luis prueba pan salado.

_______ **7.** José Luis dice que el pan dulce es horrible.

_______ **8.** El pan con ajo está demasiado caliente.

_______ **9.** Beatriz come el pan picante.

_______ **10.** La merienda de Beatriz es un asco.

Video Activities *Vocabulario*

POST-VIEWING ACTIVITY

Match the phrases from the columns below to make correct statements.

1. El pan con sal es ____.	**a.** caliente
2. El pan con azúcar es ____.	**b.** agrio
3. El pan con limón es ____.	**c.** salado
4. El pan con ajo está ____.	**d.** un asco
5. El pan con salsa es ____.	**e.** dulce
6. La merienda es ____.	**f.** picante

Nombre ______________________ Clase ______________ Fecha ______________

Video Activities *Telehistoria escena 1*

PRE-VIEWING ACTIVITY

You are going on a picnic this afternoon with some friends. Answer the following questions so you can plan properly for the picnic.

1. Who is going on the picnic with you?

____

____

2. Do you know any of your friends' favorite foods / meals? If so, what are they?

____

____

3. What would be the ideal picnic meal for you and your friends?

____

____

4. What groceries do you need to buy for this meal?

____

____

VIEWING ACTIVITY

Read through the list of groceries below before watching the video. Then, while watching the video, indicate with a checkmark (✓) which groceries José Luis and Beatriz have for the movie shoot.

________	las espinacas	________	las fresas
________	el azúcar	________	los frijoles
________	los limones	________	los tomates
________	el aceite	________	la sal
________	la mostaza	________	el carne
________	la pimienta	________	la mayonesa
________	el ajo	________	las manzanas
________	las zanahorias	________	la lechuga
________	las naranjas	________	las papas

Video Activities *Telehistoria escena 1*

POST-VIEWING ACTIVITY

Indicate whether the following statements are true (T) or false (F).

1. Hay una tortilla de patatas y un postre de fresas en la mesa. T F
2. José Luis sabe cocinar muy bien. T F
3. Beatriz piensa que José Luis hace una tortilla de patatas sabrosísima. T F
4. El tío de Beatriz es un chef. T F
5. José Luis quiere mucha fruta en la mesa. T F
6. Virginia trajo toda la comida para hoy del restaurante de tío Vicente. T F
7. José Luis es el director de la película. T F
8. Beatriz no piensa que la lechuga está muy fresca. T F

Nombre ______________________ Clase ______________ Fecha ______________

Video Activities *Telehistoria escena 2*

PRE-VIEWING ACTIVITY

Your little sister has just cooked her first three-course meal. Unfortunately, everything you try is awful! For each course listed below write a note to her, telling her the food she cooked, how it tastes, and how she can improve on the dish.

appetizer:

____

____

____

main course:

____

____

____

dessert:

____

____

____

VIEWING ACTIVITY

Read the following commands before watching the video. Then, while watching the video, indicate with a checkmark (✓) if **José Luis** makes (or might make) each imperative statement.

__________ Coma el gazpacho.

__________ Diga: «Por favor, no coman.»

__________ Prueben la tortilla y digan: «Está deliciosa.»

__________ Empiecen señor y señora Vega a comer.

__________ ¡Hiérvalas en agua!

__________ Coma las espinacas.

__________ Entonces, pruebe el postre.

__________ Beban un poco de agua, por favor.

__________ Vayan al restaurante de mi tío.

__________ Vayan a casa y regresen mañana.

Video Activities *Telehistoria escena 2*

POST-VIEWING ACTIVITY

Choose the word(s) that best complete(s) each of the following sentences.

1. Los señores Vega invitaron a los señores García a una comida en su ____.
   a. casa **b.** jardín **c.** patio
2. Los señores García son personas muy ____.
   a. importantes **b.** intelectuales **c.** organizados
3. Señor García no piensa que la tortilla está ____.
   a. sabrosa **b.** fresca **c.** salada
4. José Luis y Beatriz ____ las patatas para la tortilla.
   a. frieron **b.** batieron **c.** hirvieron
5. Señor Vega dice que la tortilla está ____.
   a. saladísima **b.** riquísima **c.** sabrosísima
6. La ensalada está un poco ____.
   a. salada **b.** dulce **c.** agria
7. La ____ no está fresca.
   a. fresa **b.** zanahoria **c.** lechuga
8. El postre está ____.
   a. dulcísimo **b.** buenísimo **c.** fresquísimo
9. Todos van a filmar la escena ____.
   a. hoy por la tarde **b.** mañana por la mañana **c.** mañana por la tarde

Nombre ______________________ Clase ______________ Fecha ______________

Video Activities *Telehistoria escena 3*

PRE-VIEWING ACTIVITY

You are giving a cooking class on your favorite recipe. Write all of the ingredients you need for this recipe. Then describe how to make the recipe, step by step.

dish:

____

ingredients:

____

____

recipe:

____

____

____

VIEWING ACTIVITY

Read the steps below for making a **tortilla de patatas** (*potato omelet*) before watching the video. Then, while you watch the video, put the steps in the correct order.

____ Fríalo todo, pero no demasiado.

____ Fríalas en el aceite caliente.

____ Bata los huevos durante dos minutos.

____ Corte las patatas y las cebollas.

____ Mezcla los huevos con las patatas y la cebolla.

____ Añada la sal.

Video Activities *Telehistoria escena 3*

POST-VIEWING ACTIVITY

Choose the word from the box that best completes each sentence.

malísima	**pimienta**	**perfecta**	**merienda**	**video**	**buenísimo**	**sal**

1. No hay ______________________ en la tortilla de patatas de José Luis y Beatriz.
2. Hay que añadir ______________________ a la tortilla después de mezclar las patatas y la cebolla.
3. José Luis y Beatriz cocinan la tortilla para el ______________________.
4. Tío Vicente come la ______________________.
5. Tío Vicente dice que la tortilla está ______________________.
6. José Luis piensa que su tortilla tiene un sabor ______________________.
7. Tío Vicente tiene un ingrediente secreto para hacer una tortilla ______________________.

Nombre ______________________ Clase ______________ Fecha ______________

Video Activities *Vocabulario*

PRE-VIEWING ACTIVITY

Put the following foods in numerical order according to your likes and dislikes. Label what you like the most (1) and the least (7). Then write a brief explanation of why you like or dislike each food.

____	chuletas de cerdo	______________________
____	filete	______________________
____	pollo asado	______________________
____	platos vegetarianos	______________________
____	el flan	______________________
____	el gazpacho	______________________
____	la tarta de chocolate	______________________

VIEWING ACTIVITY

Read the following dishes and the methods of food preparation. While you watch the video indicate with a checkmark (✓) how **tío Vicente** prepares each dish.

cocido	a la parilla	hervido	asado	frito	
____	____	____	____	____	las chuletas de cerdo
____	____	____	____	____	el filete
____	____	____	____	____	el pollo
____	____	____	____	____	el plato vegetariano
____	____	____	____	____	el flan

Nombre ______________________ Clase ______________ Fecha ______________

Video Activities *Vocabulario*

POST-VIEWING ACTIVITY

Indicate whether each of the following sentences is true (T) or false (F). If the sentence is false, correct it on the line below.

1. Tío Vicente les da una cuchara para comer las chuletas de cerdo. T F

   ____

2. Beatriz come muy fina y no necesita una servilleta. T F

   ____

3. Beatriz y José Luis no prueban los espaguetis. T F

   ____

4. Beatriz no puede comer los filetes crudos. T F

   ____

5. Santiago le trae a José Luis un plato de agua. T F

   ____

6. Tío Vicente pone caldo, tomate y huevos en su flan. T F

   ____

7. A José Luis no le gusta el gazpacho. T F

   ____

8. El restaurante tiene flan y tarta de chocolate para postre. T F

   ____

Nombre ______________________ Clase ______________ Fecha ______________

Video Activities *Telehistoria escena 1*

PRE-VIEWING ACTIVITY

Answer the following questions.

1. Have you ever had an after-school job?

____

____

2. If so, did you enjoy the job? (If not, why not?) Explain your answer.

____

____

3. What would be your ideal after-school job?

____

____

4. Why would it be an ideal after-school job?

____

____

VIEWING ACTIVITY

Read the following statements before watching the video. Then, while watching the video, indicate whether each statement is true (T) or false (F).

1. Es necesario poner la servilleta a la derecha del plato. T F
2. El tenedor va a la derecha también. T F
3. El cuchillo y la cuchara van enzima de la servilleta. T F
4. No hay que poner vasos en las mesas. T F
5. Beatriz y José Luis trabajan porque quieren más dinero para comprar ropa. T F
6. Unas de las especialidades para hoy es espaguetis. T F
7. A Beatriz le gustan los dulces. T F
8. A José Luis le encanta el gazpacho. T F

Video Activities *Telehistoria escena 1*

POST-VIEWING ACTIVITY

According to the video, who would say each of the following statements? Write (a) for **José Luis**, (b) for **Beatriz**, and (c) for **tío Vicente**.

1. ____ La cuchara siempre va al lado del cuchillo.
2. ____ ¡Yo no quiero trabajar aquí!
3. ____ Filete a la parilla y pollo asado son dos más de las especialidades de hoy.
4. ____ Me gustaría ir a una heladería.
5. ____ No tenemos bastante dinero para terminar la película.
6. ____ A mí me encantan los pasteles.
7. ____ Es muy importante tomar apuntes cuando yo hablo.
8. ____ No tenéis que comer el gazpacho, solo servirlo.
9. ____ Hay que decir: «¡Buen provecho!» a los clientes después de servir la comida.
10. ____ Comer gazpacho, ¡qué asco!

Video Activities *Telehistoria escena 2*

PRE-VIEWING ACTIVITY

Answer the following questions.

1. Name five of your favorite dishes and how each usually is cooked.

Dish:	**How food is prepared:**
__________	______________________________
__________	______________________________
__________	______________________________
__________	______________________________
__________	______________________________

2. Can each of these dishes be prepared differently than you mentioned in number one? If so, list as many different ways that each dish can be prepared.

Dish:	**How food can be prepared:**
__________	______________________________
__________	______________________________
__________	______________________________
__________	______________________________
__________	______________________________

VIEWING ACTIVITY

Read the following food items before watching the video. Then, according to what you hear in the video, indicate with a checkmark (✓) if each food or beverage is listed on the menu at **La Ermita** restaurant.

______	un filete	______	la tarta de chocolate
______	el caldo de pollo con verduras	______	refrescos
		______	el pollo asado
______	un plato vegetariano	______	té frío
______	verduras mezcladas y fritas	______	jugo de naranja
______	la paella	______	las chuletas de cerdo

Video Activities *Telehistoria escena 2*

POST-VIEWING ACTIVITY

Choose the word or phrase that best completes each sentence.

1. No hay ____ hoy.
  a. un entremés
  b. una especialidad de la casa

2. Según Beatriz las chuletas de cerdo están ____.
  a. molidas y batidas con caldo
  b. crudas

3. El filete está ____.
  a. frito en aceite
  b. crudo

4. Al cliente no le gustan ni ____ ni el plato vegetariano.
  a. el caldo de pollo con verduras
  b. el pollo asado

5. Para comer el cliente pide ____.
  a. la paella
  b. el filete a la parilla

6. El cliente no quiere ____.
  a. un refresco
  b. la paella

7. Tampoco el cliente quiere ____.
  a. té frío
  b. agua con limón

Nombre ______________________ Clase ______________ Fecha ______________

Video Activities *Telehistoria escena 3*

PRE-VIEWING ACTIVITY

Answer the following questions.

1. What is one thing you have asked a waiter to do for you?

   ____

2. List five requests that a customer might ask of a waiter.

   ____

   ____

   ____

3. Would you ever like to wait tables?

   ____

4. Why or why not?

   ____

VIEWING ACTIVITY

Read the statements below before watching the video. Then, while you watch the video, check off (✓) each statement that is equivalent to what you hear.

__________ ¡Eres un camarero excelente!

__________ Muy amable, señorita.

__________ Yo no quiero trabajar en un restaurante tampoco.

__________ ¡Buen provecho!

__________ ¿Me la puede traer la cuenta, por favor?

__________ Aquí están sus chuletas.

__________ Me la dio el señor de la mesa cinco.

Video Activities *Telehistoria escena 3*

POST-VIEWING ACTIVITY

Recall what you saw in the video and choose the most appropriate response to each question or statement.

1. Perdón, camarero. Tengo prisa. _____.
2. ¿Me puede traer el flan? _____.
3. ¿Lo compartimos? _____.
4. Beatriz, ¿me puedes ayudar con esas mesas? _____.
5. José Luis, ¿qué es eso? _____.

a. Beatriz se lo trae en seguida.
b. ¡Alguien me dio una propina de 50 euros!
c. Le traigo la cuenta a usted en seguida.
d. Sí, a mí me encanta el flan.
e. Sí, pero no quiero trabajar en un restaurante.

Nombre ______________________ Clase ______________ Fecha ______________

Video Activities *El Gran Desafío*

PRE-VIEWING ACTIVITY

Answer the following questions.

1. Do you ever help set the table at home? How do you usually set the table for dinner?

____

____

2. Briefly describe an unusual mix of foods that you like.

____

____

3. What is your favorite restaurant meal?

____

____

VIEWING ACTIVITY

Read the list of foods and tastes below. Then watch the video. Place a checkmark (✓) next to foods and tastes that are featured in **El Gran Desafío**.

__________ **1.** picante

__________ **2.** mayonesa

__________ **3.** pimienta

__________ **4.** dulce

__________ **5.** fresca

__________ **6.** sabroso

__________ **7.** vinagre

__________ **8.** ajo

__________ **9.** fresa

__________ **10.** mostaza

Nombre _______________ Clase _______________ Fecha _______________

Video Activities *El Gran Desafío*

POST-VIEWING ACTIVITY

1 Match the phrases from the columns below to make correct statements about what happened in this episode of **El Gran Desafío**.

1. El profesor Dávila ____
2. Marta ____
3. Raúl ____
4. Ana ____
5. Mónica ____

a. tiene calor.
b. cae los vasos al suelo.
c. sabe sus dos comidas.
d. pone la mesa muy rápido.
e. es colombiano y profesor.

2 Ana and Luis have won this challenge. Explain briefly why you think they won the challenge. What can you deduce about their personalities? What do you think about the other teams of Mónica and Raúl, and Marta and Carlos?

____

____

____

____

____

____

____

____

____

Video Activities Answer Key

VOCABULARIO pp. 49–50

PRE-VIEWING ACTIVITY

Answers will vary. Possible answer: My favorite meal is spaghetti with meat sauce. You have to boil the spaghetti in water. Mix the tomato sauce with meat and serve it on top of the spaghetti. I like to sprinkle cheese on top. It is delicious.

VIEWING ACTIVITY

Checkmarks: 2, 4, 5, 6, 8, 10

POST-VIEWING ACTIVITY

1. c
2. e
3. b
4. a
5. f
6. d

TELEHISTORIA ESCENA 1 pp. 51–52

PRE-VIEWING ACTIVITY

1. *Answers will vary. Possible answer:* I am going on the picnic with my friends Clara and Jody.

2. *Answers will vary. Possible answer:* Clara's favorite food is strawberries and her favorite meal is spaghetti and meatballs. Jody really likes three-cheese sandwiches.

3. *Answers will vary. Possible answer:* We would have a three-cheese sandwich, a fruit salad, and fresh lemonade.

4. *Answers will vary. Possible answer:* I would need to buy the following groceries: bread, three types of cheese, mayonnaise, salt and pepper, lettuce, strawberries, bananas, a pineapple, grapes, lemons, and sugar.

VIEWING ACTIVITY

Checkmarks: las espinacas; el aceite; la mostaza; la pimienta; las zanahorias; los tomates; la sal; la mayonesa; la lechuga

POST-VIEWING ACTIVITY

1. T
2. F
3. F
4. T
5. F
6. F
7. T
8. T

TELEHISTORIA ESCENA 2 pp. 53–54

PRE-VIEWING ACTIVITY

appetizer: *Answers will vary. Possible answer:* spinach salad: Sarah, the spinach is wilted and the tomatoes have gone bad. Next time you should get fresh vegetables for the salad.

main course: *Answers will vary. Possible answer:* spaghetti: Sarah, the spaghetti is undercooked! Next time you should keep the noodles in the boiling water for three more minutes.

dessert: *Answers will vary. Possible answer:* cake: Sarah, the cake is too dry. Next time you should add more oil and butter to the cake mix.

VIEWING ACTIVITY

Checkmarks: Coma el gazpacho. Prueben la tortilla y digan: «Está deliciosa.» Entonces, pruebe el postre. Vayan a casa y regresen mañana.

POST-VIEWING ACTIVITY

1. b
2. a
3. a
4. c
5. a
6. c
7. c
8. a
9. b

TELEHISTORIA ESCENA 3 pp. 55–56

PRE-VIEWING ACTIVITY

Answers will vary. Possible answer: **dish:** poached eggs
ingredients: two eggs, vinegar and water, butter, toast
recipe: put two teaspoons of vinegar in a full pot of water and heat until the water is boiling. Then crack the eggs and put them in the water gently with a ladle. Boil the eggs for three minutes. Then take the pot off of the heat, strain the water, and serve the eggs with butter and toast.

VIEWING ACTIVITY

Fríalo todo, pero no demasiado. 6

Fríalas en el aceite caliente. 2

Bata los huevos durante dos minutos. 3

Corte las patatas y las cebollas. 1

Mezcla los huevos con las patatas y la cebolla. 4

Añada la sal. 5

POST-VIEWING ACTIVITY

1. pimienta
2. sal
3. video
4. merienda
5. malísima
6. buenísimo
7. perfecta

VOCABULARIO pp. 57–58

PRE-VIEWING ACTIVITY

Answers will vary.

Video Activities Answer Key

VIEWING ACTIVITY

las chuletas de cerdo: frito; el filete: a la parilla; el pollo: asado; el plato vegetariano: hervido; el flan: cocido

POST-VIEWING ACTIVITY

1. F: Les da un tenedor y un cuchillo para comer las chuletas.
2. F: Beatriz pide una servilleta.
3. T
4. T
5. F: Le trae un vaso de agua.
6. F: Pone leche, azúcar, y huevos en su flan.
7. T
8. T

TELEHISTORIA ESCENA 1 pp. 59–60

PRE-VIEWING ACTIVITY

1. *Answers will vary. Possible answer:* Yes, I have had an after-school job.
2. *Answers will vary. Possible answer:* Yes, I did enjoy the job because I really liked the people I worked with and the hours were perfect for school.
3. *Answers will vary. Possible answer:* My ideal job would be delivering pizza.
4. *Answers will vary. Possible answer:* Delivering pizza is a good job because you get to drive everywhere in your own car, your schedule is flexible, and you make tips plus an hourly wage.

VIEWING ACTIVITY

1. T; **2.** F; **3.** T; **4.** F; **5.** F; **6.** T; **7.** T; **8.** F

POST-VIEWING ACTIVITY

1. c; **2.** b; **3.** c; **4.** b; **5.** a; **6.** b; **7.** c; **8.** c; **9.** c; **10.** a

TELEHISTORIA ESCENA 2 pp. 61–62

PRE-VIEWING ACTIVITY

1. *Answers will vary. Possible answer:* spaghetti / boiled; steak and eggs / the steak is grilled and the eggs are fried; hamburger / barbecued; spinach salad / cut and tossed; ice cream / frozen and on a cone
2. *Answers will vary. Possible answer:* spaghetti / baked; steak and eggs / the steak can be barbecued or pan seared and the eggs can be poached or boiled; hamburger / can be grilled; spinach salad / can be wilted in a pan and served warm; ice cream / can be lightly breaded and fried

VIEWING ACTIVITY

Checkmarks: un filete; un plato vegetariano; la paella; refrescos; el pollo asado; té frío; las chuletas de cerdo

POST-VIEWING ACTIVITY

1. b; **2.** b; **3.** a; **4.** b; **5.** a; **6.** a; **7.** a

TELEHISTORIA ESCENA 3 pp. 63–64

PRE-VIEWING ACTIVITY

1. *Answers will vary. Possible answer:* I asked my waiter to bring me some more water.
2. *Answers will vary. Possible answers:* Could you bring me some butter? Could you please bring the check? My food is cold. Could the chef reheat it? How much longer for the main course to be ready? What is the soup of the day?
3. *Answers will vary. Possible answer:* Yes I would like to wait tables.
4. *Answers will vary. Possible answer:* I would like to wait tables because I could make good money in tips.

VIEWING ACTIVITY

Checkmarks: ¡Eres un camarero excelente! Yo no quiero trabajar en un restaurante tampoco. ¡Buen provecho! ¿Me puede traer la cuenta, por favor?

POST-VIEWING ACTIVITY

1. c
2. a
3. d
4. e
5. b

EL GRAN DESAFÍO pp. 65–66

PRE-VIEWING ACTIVITY

1. *Answers will vary.*
2. *Answers will vary.*
3. *Answers will vary.*

VIEWING ACTIVITY

Checkmarks: 2, 3, 4, 6, 9, 10

EL GRAN DESAFÍO p. 66

POST-VIEWING ACTIVITY

1

1. e
2. a
3. b
4. d
5. c

2 *Answers will vary.*

UNIDAD 5 Lección 2

Video Activities Answer Key

Video Scripts

VOCABULARIO

Beatriz: ¡Hola! Me llamo Beatriz y éste es mi mejor amigo...

José Luis: José Luis.

Beatriz: Tenemos hambre pero es muy tarde para comer.

José Luis: Y demasiado temprano para cenar.

Beatriz: Entonces estoy preparando una merienda aquí, en la cocina del restaurante de mi tío Vicente.

José Luis: ¿Estás cocinando? ¿Qué estás haciendo?

Beatriz: ¿Ves? Estoy hirviendo unas zanahorias. Ahora frío el ajo y la cebolla en el aceite. Aquí tengo la mostaza y el vinagre. Primero los mezclo, y luego añado la sal y la pimienta. También bato unos huevos y añado las espinacas.

José Luis: ¿Pero qué estás cocinando? ¿Ésta es tu receta? ¡Parece que estás mezclando tres recetas en una!

Beatriz: ¡Es una sorpresa!

José Luis: ¿Tengo que probarlo?

Beatriz: Sí, sí. Te gusta probarlo todo, ¿no? Conozco un juego divertido. Yo pongo un ingrediente en el pan y tú dices qué sabor tiene.

José Luis: Vale.

Beatriz: Cierra los ojos. ¿Qué sabor tiene?

José Luis: Bueno, está salado... Pusiste sal.

Beatriz: Muy bien. Ahora éste.

José Luis: Está muy dulce. Pusiste azúcar. Está delicioso. ¡Agh! Está agrio. ¡Es...limón! Oh.

Beatriz: Muy bien. Ahora, éste.

José Luis: Está demasiado caliente.

Beatriz: Perdón. Ahora... ¿Picante? ¡Qué asco!

TELEHISTORIA ESCENA 1

Beatriz: ¡Todo está bellísimo!

José Luis: Sí. Los actores están arreglándose para la escena. Vamos a ver si está todo: la tortilla de patatas, el postre de fresas...

Beatriz: Una tortilla de patatas, ¿tú sabes cocinar?

José Luis: Sí, un poco.

Beatriz: Mi tío Vicente, el chef, hace una tortilla de patatas sabrosísima.

José Luis: Juan, quiero muchas verduras en la mesa. Necesitamos mucho color: espinacas, zanahorias, tomates...

Beatriz: Mira, Virginia llegó del supermercado. Gracias. Aceite, mostaza, mayonesa, pimienta, sal, lechuga...

José Luis: Esa lechuga, ¿está fresca?

Beatriz: ¡Fresquísima! Allí está todo, señor director. ¿Empezamos?

José Luis: Sí. Pero, ¿la lechuga está fresca?

TELEHISTORIA ESCENA 2

José Luis: Bueno. Los señores Vega invitaron a los señores García a una comida en su jardín. Los señores García son personas muy importantes. Vamos a empezar. Primero, usted, señora Vega, sirva el gazpacho a la señora García y diga: «Por favor, coman.» Entonces, señor y señora García: prueben la tortilla y digan: «Está deliciosa.» Después, empiecen todos a comer. ¿Vale? ¡Acción!

Video Scripts

Sra. Vega: Por favor, coman.

Sra. García: ¡Está deliciosa!

Sr. García: ¡No! No está sabrosa. ¿Frieron las patatas para la tortilla?

José Luis: Eh..., corte. No, las hervimos... en agua.

Sr. Vega: ¡Está saladísima! ¡Qué asco!

José Luis: Entonces, no coma la tortilla, señor Vega. Coma la ensalada... es de lechuga, tomate y cebolla! ¡Está fresquísima!

Sr. Vega: Perdón...pero la ensalada está un poco agria. Tiene demasiado vinagre. Y la lechuga no está fresca.

José Luis: Entonces, prueben el postre, ¡es de fresas! Está dulce y sabroso.

Sra. Vega: Tiene demasiado azúcar. ¡Está dulcísimo!

Beatriz: Beban un poco de agua, por favor.

Sra. Vega: Estos chicos... ¡no cocinan nada bien!

Beatriz: Esperen un momento. No coman más, por favor. José Luis, necesitamos ayuda. Vamos al restaurante de mi tío, ¿vale?

José Luis: Señoras, señores, vamos a filmar la escena mañana. Por favor, vayan a casa, y regresen mañana a las siete de la mañana.

Sra. García: Pero... ¡está todo delicioso!

TELEHISTORIA ESCENA 3

José Luis: Ahora vamos a usar una receta. «Ingredientes: aceite, cuatro patatas grandes, una cebolla grande, cuatro huevos y sal. Primero, corte las patatas y la cebolla..., fríalas despacio en el aceite caliente. Bata los huevos, mézclelos con las patatas y la cebolla, y añada la sal. Fríalo, pero no lo cocine demasiado.»

Tío Vicente: ¿Qué estáis haciendo?

Beatriz: Estamos preparando una tortilla de patatas, tío Vicente...para el video. ¿Y tú?

Tío Vicente: Estoy comiendo la merienda.

José Luis: Pruébela. ¿No tiene un sabor buenísimo?

Tío Vicente: No. ¡Está malísima!

Santiago: «Bata los huevos durante dos minutos...»

Tío Vicente: ¿Queréis saber el ingrediente secreto para hacer una tortilla de patatas perfecta?

José Luis: Perdón, repítalo, por favor. ¿Cuál es el ingrediente secreto?

José Luis y Beatriz: Gracias.

Video Scripts

VOCABULARIO

José Luis: Beatriz y yo queremos saber más sobre cómo preparar una buena comida. Estamos en el restaurante del tío de Beatriz, tío Vicente. Perdón...el CHEF Vicente.

Beatriz: Éste es el chef Vicente Cruz. Y éste es su restaurante.

José Luis: ¿Cúal es la especialidad de la casa, señor Cruz?

Tío Vicente: Las chuletas de cerdo están muy buenas.

Beatriz: ¿Cómo las cocináis?

Tío Vicente: Las servimos fritas. Debéis probarlas. Santiago, ¿me traes cuchillos y tenedores, por favor? Un cuchillo y un tenedor para vosotros. ¡Buen provecho!

Beatriz: Necesito una servilleta.

Tío Vicente: Santiago, una servilleta, por favor. Esta noche también tenemos espaguetis. Otra especialidad es el filete a la parrilla.

Beatriz: ¿Puedo probarlos?

Tío Vicente: Ésos están crudos. Pero éste no está crudo. ¿Queréis probar éste?

Beatriz: ¡Qué rico!

José Luis: ¡Excelente! Por favor... ¿Me puede dar un vaso de agua?

Tío Vicente: Santiago, un vaso de agua, por favor. Esta noche tenemos también pollo asado...Y paella. Ah, y un delicioso plato vegetariano...de zanahorias hervidas, con arroz. Santiago está haciendo un flan.

José Luis: Me gusta mucho el flan. ¿Cómo lo preparan?

Tío Vicente: Con huevos, leche y azúcar. Añadimos la leche a los huevos batidos, todo bien mezclado con el azúcar. Debe estar bien cocido. ¿Queréis probarlo? Y de entremés tenemos gazpacho.

José Luis: ¿Gazpacho? ¡No me gusta!

Tío Vicente: Aquí tenéis una cuchara. ¿Queréis probarlo?

José Luis: Está delicioso.

Beatriz: Sí...¡Delicioso!

Tío Vicente: Y de postre, tenemos tarta de chocolate, ¿queréis probarla?

José Luis: ¡Por favor!

Tío Vicente: Santiago, tarta de chocolate, por favor.

TELEHISTORIA ESCENA 1

Tío Vicente: Debéis poner la servilleta aquí. El tenedor va a la izquierda. El cuchillo va encima de la servilleta. La cuchara al lado del cuchillo. Y...el vaso aquí.

Beatriz: ¿Por qué estamos trabajando aquí?

José Luis: ¡Porque necesitamos más dinero para terminar la película!

Tío Vicente: A escribir...

Beatriz: ¿Por qué no trabajamos en una heladería? ¡Así, mientras trabajamos, podemos comer helado.

Tío Vicente: A escribir. Las especialidades para hoy son: filete a la parrilla, pollo asado y espaguetis.

Beatriz: O en una pastelería. ¡Mmmm!

Tío Vicente: De entremés, tenemos gazpacho. Tenéis que servirlo. No tenéis que comerlo.

Beatriz: Muy amable, gracias.

Video Scripts

TELEHISTORIA ESCENA 2

Cliente 1: ¿Nadie trabaja aquí? ¿Cuál es la especialidad de la casa?

Beatriz: Ninguna. Pero las chuletas de cerdo están muy buenas.

Cliente 1: ¿Cómo las preparan?

Beatriz: Las preparan...o hervidas en caldo, o molidas y batidas con huevo. No. Perdón. Están crudas.

Cliente 1: ¿Y el filete? ¿También está crudo?

Beatriz: Lo preparan frito en aceite con algo...alguna verdura, creo.

Cliente 1: No me gusta ni el pollo asado ni el plato vegetariano. Me gustaría la paella.

Beatriz: ¡Excelente! ¿Y para beber? ¿Un refresco?

Cliente 1: No, gracias.

Beatriz: ¿Tal vez un té frío con limón?

Cliente 1: No, tampoco. Nada, gracias.

Beatriz: Muy bien. Perdone. ¿Qué pidió?

Cliente 1: ¡LA PAELLA! ¡LA PAELLA!

TELEHISTORIA ESCENA 3

José Luis: Aquí están sus filetes. ¡Buen provecho!

Cliente 2: Necesito la cuenta. ¿Me la puede traer, por favor? Tengo prisa.

Cliente 3: Por favor, ¿me puede traer el flan? ¿Lo compartimos?

Cliente 4: Perdón. Muchas gracias por atendernos. ¡Eres muy atento, y un camarero excelente!

José Luis: Beatriz, ésta es la cuenta del señor de la mesa cinco. ¿Se la puedes dar? Y en la mesa dos quieren un flan. ¿Se lo puedes servir?

Beatriz: No quiero trabajar en un restaurante.

José Luis: Ni yo tampoco. Es un trabajo muy difícil.

Beatriz: ¿Qué podemos hacer? ¿Alguien te dio una buena propina?

José Luis: Sí...me la dieron unas señoras muy simpáticas.

Beatriz: ¿Te podemos ayudar?

COMPARACÍON CULTURAL VIDEO

LEVEL 2 UNIT 5 GRAN DESAFÍO

Profesor Dávila: ¡Hola a todos y bienvenidos al Gran Desafío! Yo soy Miguel Dávila. Soy colombiano y soy profesor de historia contemporánea en la Universidad Nacional Autónoma de México. Yo voy estar con ustedes durante los primeros cuatro desafíos. Cada desafío tiene un punto. El equipo que gana más puntos, va a participar en la competencia final, junto a los ganadores de otros países. El premio de la competencia final será un año de estudios en la Universidad Nacional Autónoma de México, un apartamento en el D.F. y 100,000.00 pesos para gastos por un año. ¿Alguna pregunta? ¿Marta? ¿Tienes alguna pregunta?

Video Scripts

Marta: Profesor, hace calor. No estoy bien. No quiero estar aquí. ¿Podemos ir a otro lugar?

Profesor Dávila: Un momento Marta, primero debemos seleccionar los equipos. Tomen agua.

Marta: No. Gracias.

Profesor Dávila: Ahora tomen un papel. El número en el papel les dice en qué equipo van a estar.

Luis: ¿Quiere saber qué número tengo?

Profesor Dávila: Sí. Díselo a todo el grupo.

Luis: Uno.

Profesor Dávila: ¡Excelente! Ahora hagan los equipos. Bueno jóvenes, ¿están listos? Entonces los equipos son Luis y Ana, Marta y Carlos, y Raúl y Mónica. Ahora sí, podemos continuar. Vamos al restaurante El Rincón Tarasco para comenzar nuestro primer desafío.

Don Pedro: Buenos días. Usted debe ser el profesor Dávila.

Profesor Dávila: Sí. ¿Usted es Don Pedro? Mucho gusto. Ellos son Raúl, Ana, Luis, Mónica, Marta y Carlos.

Don Pedro: Es un placer chicos. Bienvenidos. Ya está listo todo. Sigan por aquí. Yo voy en un momento.

Profesor Dávila: Jóvenes, en este desafío tenemos dos partes. En la primera parte, deben correr con platos, vasos, cuchillos, cucharas, tenedores, servilletas, para preparar una mesa para cuatro personas. El equipo que lleva todo en menos tiempo gana. Aquí tienen todo ¿Listos? ¡Adelante! ¿Listos?

Todos: ¡Sí!

Profesor Dávila: ¡Ya! Terminamos. Felicitaciones Ana, lo hiciste muy bien. Muy bien, ahora estamos listos para nuestra segunda parte. Ahora van a probar varios platos de comida y decir qué son. ¿Listos? La primera eres tú, Marta. ¡Buen provecho!

Marta: ¡Qué asco! Uy, no me gustó. ¿Qué me dieron?

Profesor Dávila: Marta, simplemente era flan con un poco de mayonesa y pimienta. Ahora tú, Mónica. ¿Lista? ¡Buen provecho!

Mónica: Um. El sabor fuerte era de sopa de tomate. ¿Es sopa azteca? Y hay algo dulce.

Raúl: ¡Bien!

Profesor Dávila: Sí.

Mónica: Era chocolate. Creo que era pastel de chocolate.

Video Scripts

Profesor Dávila: ¡Muy bien Mónica! Y ahora tú Luis. ¿Listo? ¡Buen provecho!

Luis: Um. Sabroso. Es dulce, agrio y un poco salado. Es fresa, con mostaza y un poco de sal.

Profesor Dávila: Bueno Luis. Bueno chicos, el equipo ganador de este desafío es el equipo uno, Ana y Luis. ¡Felicitaciones!

Don Pedro: Ahora, coman las especialidades de la casa. ¡Y la casa invita! Nos puede traer las chuletas de puerco y el pollo asado. Y traiga de postre el pastel de chocolate, ¡pero sin sopa azteca por favor!

Audio Scripts

UNIDAD 5, LECCIÓN 1
TEXTBOOK SCRIPTS
TXT CD 6

PRESENTACIÓN DE VOCABULARIO

Level 2 Textbook pp. 254–255

TXT CD 6, Track 1

A. ¡Hola! Soy José Luis y voy a entrar en este supermercado porque aquí venden las verduras y frutas más frescas. Más tarde, Beatriz y yo vamos a preparar una comida deliciosa.

B. Beatriz bate los huevos para una tortilla de patatas. Los ingredientes son: patatas, cebolla, huevos y sal. Y claro, ella necesita el aceite para cocinarla. Para preparar la ensalada voy a mezclar el aceite con el vinagre y un poco de limón. Lo añado a la ensalada con sal y pimienta. Siempre pruebo la comida. ¡Qué deliciosa!

C. Hay ingredientes necesarios en la cocina como el azúcar para los postres y la mayonesa y la mostaza para los sándwiches. Es necesario saber cómo cocinar los ingredientes. Por ejemplo, los puedes freír en aceite caliente o hervir en agua. Ahora, frío la cebolla y hiervo las zanahorias.

D. Todas las comidas tienen sabor. ¿Cuál es el sabor que prefieres? ¿Algo agrio como un limón o dulce como el chocolate? ¿Algo picante como la mostaza o algo salado como las patatas fritas? Para ti, ¿cuál es la comida más deliciosa?

¡A RESPONDER!

Level 2 Textbook p. 255

TXT CD 6, Track 2

Escucha las siguientes frases. Decide si habla del sabor de una comida o de cómo preparar la comida. Levanta la mano derecha si es un sabor. Levanta la mano izquierda si es cómo preparar algo.

1. Es muy dulce.
2. Tiene que freírlos.
3. Es picante.
4. Vamos a añadirlos.
5. ¿Te parece salado?
6. ¡Qué agrio!
7. ¿Puedes hervirlas?
8. Hay que mezclarlos.

TELEHISTORIA ESCENA 1

Level 2 Textbook p. 257

TXT CD 6, Track 3

Beatriz: ¡Todo está bellísimo!

José Luis: Sí. Los actores están arreglándose para la escena. Vamos a ver si está todo: la tortilla de patatas, el postre de fresas…

Beatriz: Una tortilla de patatas. ¿Tú sabes cocinar?

José Luis: Sí, un poco.

Beatriz: Mi tío Vicente, el chef, hace una tortilla de patatas sabrosísima.

José Luis: Juan, quiero muchas verduras en la mesa. Necesitamos mucho color: espinacas, zanahorias, tomates...

Beatriz: Mira, Virginia llegó del supermercado. Gracias. Aceite, mostaza, mayonesa, pimienta, sal, lechuga...

José Luis: Esa lechuga, ¿está fresca?

Beatriz: ¡Fresquísima! Allí está todo, señor director. ¿Empezamos?

José Luis: Sí. Pero, ¿la lechuga está fresca?

ACTIVIDAD 7 - UNAS ESPINACAS DELICIOSAS

Level 2 Textbook p. 260

TXT CD 6, Track 4

Escucha lo que dice el cocinero y pon los pasos de la receta en orden.

Tío Vicente: Estas espinacas son fáciles de preparar y siempre salen sabrosas. Primero, hierva las espinacas frescas en agua salada. Luego, fría el ajo en aceite y fría la cebolla con el ajo. Añada las espinacas. Luego, añada pimienta y un poco de limón. Mezcle bien todos los ingredientes. Pruebe las espinacas antes de servirlas. Mmmmm. ¡Estas espinacas están riquísimas! Finalmente, sirva el plato bien caliente.

PRONUNCIACIÓN

Level 2 Textbook p. 261

TXT CD 6, Track 5

La letra **d**

The Spanish **d** can have a hard sound or a soft sound. At the beginning of a sentence, after a pause, or after the letters **l** or **n**, the **d** has a hard sound like the **d** of the English word *day*. In all other cases, the **d** sounds like the soft *th* sound of the English word *the*.

Listen to and repeat these phrases, noticing the soft and hard sounds of **d**.

Daniela, ¿vas al merca**d**o?

¡La merien**d**a está **d**eliciosa!

A**d**iós, Davi**d**.

Nos vemos el **d**omingo.

TELEHISTORIA ESCENA 2

Level 2 Textbook p. 262

TXT CD 6, Track 6

José Luis: Bueno. Los señores Vega invitaron a los señores García a una comida en su jardín. Los señores García son personas muy importantes. ¿Vale? ¡Acción!

Sra. Vega: Por favor, coman.

Sra. García: ¡Está deliciosa!

Sr. García: ¡No! No está sabrosa. ¿Frieron las patatas para la tortilla?

José Luis: Corte. No. Las hervimos... en agua.

Sr. Vega: ¡Está saladísima! ¡Qué asco!

José Luis: Entonces, no coma la tortilla, señora Vega. Coma la ensalada...

Sr. Vega: Perdón... pero la ensalada está un poco agria. Tiene demasiado vinagre. Y la lechuga no está fresca.

Beatriz: Beban un poco de agua, por favor.

Sra. Vega: ¡Estos chicos no cocinan nada bien!

Beatriz: Esperen un momento. No coman más, por favor. José Luis, necesitamos ayuda. Vamos al restaurante de mi tío, ¿vale?

José Luis: Señoras, señores, vamos a filmar la escena mañana. Por favor, vayan a casa, y regresen mañana a las siete de la mañana.

Sra. García: Pero... ¡está todo delicioso!

TELEHISTORIA COMPLETA

Level 2 Textbook p. 267

TXT CD 6, Track 7

Escena 1 Resumen José Luis y Beatriz se preparan para filmar su película. Ponen una mesa con mucha comida que preparó José Luis.

Escena 2 Resumen En la escena, los actores están comiendo. Prueban algunos platos, pero todos están horribles. No pueden terminar la escena.

Escena 3

José Luis: Ahora vamos a usar una receta. «Ingredientes: aceite, cuatro patatas grandes, una cebolla grande, cuatro huevos y sal». «Primero, corte las patatas y las cebollas. Fríalas despacio en el aceite caliente».

José Luis: «Bata los huevos, mézclelos con las patatas y la cebolla, y añada la sal. Fríalo, pero no lo cocine demasiado».

Tío Vicente: ¿Qué estáis haciendo?

Beatriz: Estamos preparando una tortilla de patatas, tío Vicente, para el video. ¿Y tú?

Tío Vicente: Estoy comiendo la merienda.

José Luis: Pruébela. ¿No tiene un sabor buenísimo?

Tío Vicente: No. ¡Está malísima! ¿Queréis saber el ingrediente secreto para hacer una tortilla perfecta?

José Luis: Perdón, repítalo por favor. ¿Cuál es el ingrediente secreto?

ACTIVIDAD 20 - INTEGRACIÓN

Level 2 Textbook p. 269

TXT CD 6, Track 8

Lee la lista de ingredientes y escucha el programa «Cocinando con Nacho». Luego da instrucciones para preparar una ensalada con vinagreta para la cena.

FUENTE 2

TXT CD 6, Track 9

Listen and take notes.

¿Es difícil hacer la vinagreta?

¿Cuándo debes prepararla?

¿Qué ingredientes recomienda Nacho para la ensalada?

Es fácil hacer una vinagreta sabrosísima. Primero, mezcle bien la mostaza con la sal, la pimienta y el vinagre rojo. Añada el aceite lentamente y bátalo bien con la mostaza y el vinagre. Al final, corte el ajo y la cebolla y añádalos con el zumo de limón. Mézclelo todo. Y ya está la vinagreta, pero es bueno hacerla una hora antes de servirla,

Audio Scripts

o más. Si usted la sirve antes, la cebolla y el ajo van a estar demasiado picantes. Entonces, después de una hora, sírvala con una ensalada de lechuga o espinacas y tomate. Si quiere, hierva y corte un huevo y añádalo también. Mmm... ¡Riquísimo!

REPASO: ACTIVIDAD 1 - LISTEN AND UNDERSTAND

Level 2 Textbook p. 274

TXT CD 6, Track 10

Escucha una receta para ensaladilla rusa: una ensalada de patatas con mayonesa. ¿Qué debes hacer con los ingredientes en cada paso? Escribe el verbo o los verbos apropiados y escribe mandatos.

1. Hierva las patatas y la zanahoria en agua por diez minutos. Luego sáquelas del agua y póngalas a un lado.
2. Corte una cebolla muy pequeña.
3. Para preparar la mayonesa, mezcle el aceite, un huevo, dos cucharas de vinagre y sal. Bata todos los ingredientes para la mayonesa por unos minutos.
4. Para hacer la ensalada, mezcle las patatas y las zanahorias con la mayonesa.
5. Pruebe la ensalada y añada sal si es necesario.
6. Ponga la ensalada de patatas en un plato grande.
7. Para decorar la ensalada añada un huevo cocido y cortado, la cebolla cortada y pimienta roja.
8. Sírvala fría.

WORKBOOK SCRIPTS
WB CD 3

INTEGRACIÓN HABLAR

Level 2 Workbook p. 206

WB CD 3, Track 1

Escucha el mensaje telefónico que le dejó Martina a su amigo Gustavo. Toma apuntes.

FUENTE 2

WB CD 3, Track 2

Martina: Hola, Gustavo. ¿Jimena y tú pueden ir al supermercado? Compren seis huevos, patatas, cebollas y zanahorias. Voy a preparar una receta de huevos con verduras. Pero quiero hacerla más sabrosa. Por favor, compren espinacas y ajo. Voy a añadirlos a la receta. ¡Ah! Además, necesito pimienta y aceite para esta receta. ¡Gracias!

INTEGRACIÓN ESCRIBIR

Level 2 Workbook p. 207

WB CD 3, Track 3

Escucha el anuncio en la radio sobre la competencia. Toma apuntes.

FUENTE 2

WB CD 3, Track 4

Vengan a participar en la competencia de la Escuela de Cocina López. Si saben cocinar comidas sabrosas, entonces pueden ganar. Si no tienen una receta, no importa, ¡escriban una! No es muy difícil. Piensen en cómo van juntos los diferentes sabores y ya. Es facilísimo. Por ejemplo, pueden preparar recetas de sopa con verduras frescas. Visítenos este fin de semana en el Centro Comercial Macarena.

ESCUCHAR A, ACTIVIDAD 1

Level 2 Workbook p. 208

WB CD 3, Track 5

Escucha a Lorenzo. Encierra en un círculo las cosas que tiene que comprar en el supermercado.

Lorenzo: Hoy voy al supermercado. Mi mamá necesita algunas cosas y mi hermana no puede ir. Tengo que comprar fresas, cebollas, zanahorias, huevos, leche, azúcar, sal y mayonesa. Siempre le pido a mi mamá más postres porque me encantan las cosas dulces. Pero ella prepara más cosas saladas que dulces

ESCUCHAR A, ACTIVIDAD 2

Level 2 Workbook p. 208

WB CD 3, Track 6

Escucha la conversación entre Daniela y su mamá. Contesta las preguntas.

Mamá: Daniela, ¿puedes ir al supermercado?

Daniela: No, lo siento mamá, no puedo. Tengo que terminar el postre de chocolate para Pedro.

Mamá: Tu hermano tampoco quiere ir. Sean buenos con su madre. Necesito muchas cosas. Yo no tengo tiempo porque tengo mucho trabajo.

Daniela: No, no, yo no puedo. Vayan ustedes. Pedro llega en una hora y todavía no termino su postre. ¿Por qué no puede ir Lorenzo?

Mamá: Porque hoy sale con sus amigos.

Daniela: Bueno, puede ir rápido y volver a tiempo.

ESCUCHAR B, ACTIVIDAD 1

Level 2 Workbook p. 209

WB CD 3, Track 7

Escucha la conversación de Luciana y Lucas. Luego, subraya una vez lo que come Luciana y dos veces lo que come Lucas.

Luciana: Lucas, ¿qué estás comiendo?

Lucas: Estoy comiendo una ensalada de lechuga y unas fresas frescas muy dulces, ¡están deliciosas! Y tú, ¿qué comes?

Luciana: Yo como una tortilla de patatas. Mi mamá hace tortillas de patatas muy ricas. Es una receta de la abuela de la abuela de mi abuela... es decir, es una receta muy vieja. También como una ensalada de tomate con mucho ajo.

Lucas: ¿Te gustan las cosas picantes? Yo no como mostaza porque no me gustan las cosas picantes.

Luciana: A mí sí me gustan. Pero también como cosas dulces. Ahora voy a comer un chocolate.

Lucas: A mí también me gustan los dulces. Yo voy a comer un plátano.

ESCUCHAR B, ACTIVIDAD 2

Level 2 Workbook p. 209

WB CD 3, Track 8

Escucha lo que dice Norma. Luego, completa las siguientes oraciones.

Norma: Las verduras son muy buenas. Pueden prepararlas de muchas maneras. Me encantan las patatas. Mézclenlas con cebollas y huevos y tienen una tortilla deliciosa. Compren tomates y lechuga, córtenlos pequeñitos, añádanles aceite, sal y limón y ya tienen una ensalada muy rica. ¡Me encantan las verduras!

ESCUCHAR C, ACTIVIDAD 1

Level 2 Workbook p. 210

WB CD 3, Track 9

Escucha la conversación telefónica entre Malena y Juan Carlos. Toma apuntes. Luego completa las oraciones.

Malena: Juan Carlos, tengo un problema: mi hermano y yo tenemos que preparar la comida hoy. ¡Pero no sabemos preparar nada!

Juan Carlos: Estén tranquilos. Hay muchas cosas fáciles de hacer. ¿Les gusta la tortilla? ¿Les gusta la sopa de verduras? ¿Les gusta la ensalada de tomates?

Malena: Sí, nos gustan las comidas saladas, no nos gustan agrias o picantes.

Juan Carlos: Entonces no les añadan limón a la ensalada o pimienta a la comida. Añádanle sólo sal y aceite.

Malena: ¿Puedes ayudarnos?

Juan Carlos: Sí. Vayan al supermercado a comprar los ingredientes de la comida. Después vengan a mi casa.

ESCUCHAR C, ACTIVIDAD 2

Level 2 Workbook p. 210

WB CD 3, Track 10

Escucha lo que dice Dante y toma apuntes. Luego, contesta las preguntas con oraciones completas.

Dante: Mi hermano y yo preparamos la comida porque hoy mi mamá trabaja fuera de la ciudad. No sabemos hacer nada, ¡ni freír un huevo! Mi hermano está hablando por teléfono con su amigo Juan Carlos, que tiene un restaurante y sabe mucho de cocina. Mi hermano tiene que decirle que no nos gustan las cosas picantes. Tal vez piensa en ayudarnos con algo con pimienta o ajo. ¡Qué asco!

Audio Scripts

ASSESSMENT SCRIPTS
LESSON 1 TEST: ESCUCHAR

Modified Assessment Book p. 170

On-level Assessment Book p. 221

Pre-AP Assessment Book p. 170

ACTIVIDAD A

TEST CD 2, Track 1

Escucha el siguiente audio. Luego, completa la actividad A.

Pepe Machado: Buenos días. Hoy voy a preparar una ensalada de lechuga y fresas muy fácil y sabrosa. Éstos son los ingredientes que necesita usted:

1 lechuga fresca

8 fresas

1 cebolla

2 zanahorias

aceite, vinagre, mostaza y pimienta

Lave y corte la lechuga, las fresas, la cebolla y las zanahorias. Mézclelas. Entonces bata el aceite, el vinagre, la mostaza y la pimienta. Añada la mezcla a la lechuga, las fresas, las cebollas y las zanahorias. Sé que le va a gustar a usted. ¡Buen provecho!

ACTIVIDAD B

Modified Assessment Book p. 170

On-level Assessment Book p. 221

Pre-AP Assessment Book p. 170

TEST CD 2, Track 2

Escucha el siguiente audio. Luego, completa la actividad B.

Mamá: Paqui, ¿puedes ir al supermercado? Necesito algunas cosas para la cena esta noche.

Paqui: ¡Claro que sí! ¿Qué necesitas?

Mamá: Necesito carne para hacer hamburguesas; patatas para freír; y espinacas, zanahorias y tomates para hacer una ensalada.

Paqui; ¿Compro el postre?

Mamá: No, ya tenemos postre, pero necesito pan.

Paqui: Bien, entonces paso por la panadería.

Mamá: Gracias, hija.

HERITAGE LEARNER SCRIPTS
HL CDs 2 & 5

INTEGRACIÓN HABLAR

Level 2 HL Workbook p. 208

HL CD 2, Track 1

Escucha las recomendaciones de un cocinero sobre cómo preparar una buena paella valenciana. Toma notas mientras escuchas y luego completa la actividad.

FUENTE 2
HL CD 2, Track 2

Una paellera es una cazuela grande, poco honda, con asas. Necesita también una cuchara de palo para remover todos los ingredientes mientras cocina. Nunca sustituya el aceite de oliva por otro tipo de aceite, el aceite de oliva le da un sabor especial a la cocina española. Y aunque es caro, siempre es importante conseguir el azafrán, que le da ese color amarillo a la paella. Otro consejo importante, no remueva el arroz una vez que está hirviendo. Déjelo tranquilo para que no se reblandezca.

INTEGRACIÓN ESCRIBIR

Level 2 HL Workbook p. 209

HL CD 2, Track 3

Escucha el mensaje que la señora Estela Pérez dejó para su hijo José Arturo. Toma notas mientras escuchas. Luego completa la actividad.

FUENTE 2
HL CD 2, Track 4

José Arturo, ¿estás en casa, hijo? ... Mira que necesito un favor urgente. Estoy en casa de Pilar y olvidé la receta de la ensalada en el tablero de magnetos, junto al refrigerador. Sé bueno y llámame a casa de tu tía. Ya sabes que con la memoria que tengo no me acuerdo de nada. Espero, pues... Ah, y no se te olvide que me debes la receta de la ensalada que preparaste ayer. Te quedó riquísima, hijo. Eres un genio.

LESSON 1 TEST: ESCUCHAR, ACTIVIDAD A

HL Assessment Book p. 176

HL CD 4, Track 1

Con la ayuda de Patricia, Carlos preparó una cena para sus amigos. Escucha su conversación y contesta las preguntas usando oraciones completas.

Miguel: ¡Hummmm! ¡Qué bien huele!

Ana: ¡Y qué bien luce! ¡Qué colorido!

Carlos: Les preparé una cena de tapas españolas. Muy informal.

Miguel: ¡Tapas! ¡Qué buena idea! ¡Así podremos probar varios platos en pequeñas cantidades! ¿Cómo se te ocurrió?

Carlos: Recuerden que mi madre es española. Estos platos los conozco muy bien desde que era niño.

Ana: Explícanos de qué trata cada cosa, Carlos. Esta ensalada, por ejemplo, parece deliciosa.

Carlos: Se llama «ensaladilla» y lleva patatas, zanahorias, guisantes, atún y mayonesa.

Ana: ¿Preparaste tú mismo la mayonesa o usaste una comercial?

Carlos: Todo lo preparé yo mismo.

Miguel: ¿Preparaste la mayonesa con vinagre?

Carlos: No, le puse limón. Es un poquito más agrio que el vinagre pero le da un sabor más rico a la mayonesa.

Miguel: ¿Y esto, Carlos, qué es?

Carlos: Es la famosa tortilla de patatas: patatas, cebollas y huevos, más algún secreto que no les diré.

Ana: ¡Cuántas delicias! ¡Es realmente una mesa española! ¡Ya quiero comenzar!

Carlos: ¡Pues sírvanse!

ACTIVIDAD B

HL Assessment Book p. 176

HL CD 4, Track 2

Escucha con atención y luego completa el texto con las oraciones faltantes.

Speaker: Carlos quiere ser chef y Patricia comparte con él su gusto por la cocina española. Este fin de semana Patricia ayudó a Carlos a preparar una cena para los amigos. Por la mañana ella fue al supermercado y compró los ingredientes necesarios. Puso mucha atención en que todo estuviera fresquísimo. Luego se encargó de pelar y freír las patatas y la cebolla para la tortilla y de batir los huevos. También quiso hervir los vegetales para la ensaladilla y mezclar todo con la mayonesa antes de que Carlos le diera el toque final. Ella estuvo atenta al sabor de cada cosa, para que nada resultara demasiado salado o demasiado picante. No fue necesario usar una receta porque Carlos conoce muy bien la preparación de cada plato. Los amigos estuvieron encantados. No se cansaban de probar todo una y otra vez. Todo les pareció riquísimo y agradecieron a Carlos y a Patricia por la invitación.

Audio Scripts

UNIDAD 5, LECCIÓN 2
TXT CD 6

PRESENTACIÓN DE VOCABULARIO

Level 2 Textbook pp. 278–279

TXT CD 6, Track 11

A. **José Luis:** Estamos en el restaurante del tío Vicente. El camarero es muy atento. Nos trae el menú y pedimos. Beatriz pide la paella y yo pido un plato vegetariano, los espaguetis. Es una especialidad de la casa. Todo parece riquísimo.

B. **José Luis:** De entremés pedimos el gazpacho. Es una sopa fría de tomates y otras verduras frescas, mezcladas y molidas. Para prepararla, usas verduras crudas, no cocidas.

C. **José Luis:** Hay más especialidades en este restaurante. A nosotros nos encantan el filete a la parrilla, el pollo asado y las chuletas de cerdo. ¡Son muy deliciosos!

D. **José Luis:** ¿Qué pedimos de postre? ¿El flan o la tarta de chocolate? ¿Y un té para beber?

E. **José Luis:** ¿Por qué no vamos a otro lugar para el postre? Podemos ir a una heladería para comer helado o a una pastelería para pasteles. ¡Vamos!

¡A RESPONDER!

Level 2 Textbook p. 279

TXT CD 6, Track 12

Escucha esta lista de palabras. Levanta la mano derecha si es una comida. Levanta la mano izquierda si es un objeto que usas para comer.

1. la paella
2. el flan
3. la cuchara
4. el caldo
5. el cuchillo
6. el gazpacho
7. la servilleta
8. el tenedor

TELEHISTORIA ESCENA 1

Level 2 Textbook p. 281

TXT CD 6, Track 13

Tío Vicente: Debéis poner la servilleta aquí. El tenedor va a la izquierda. El cuchillo va encima de la servilleta. La cuchara al lado del cuchillo. Y... el vaso aquí.

Beatriz: ¿Por qué estamos trabajando aquí?

José Luis: ¡Porque necesitamos más dinero para terminar la película!

Tío Vicente: A escribir...

Beatriz: ¿Por qué no trabajamos en una heladería? ¡Así, mientras trabajamos, podemos comer helado!

Tío Vicente: A escribir. Las especialidades para hoy son: filete a la parrilla, pollo asado y espaguetis.

Beatriz: O en una pastelería. ¡Mmmm!

Tío Vicente: De entremés tenemos gazpacho. Tenéis que servirlo. No tenéis que comerlo.

Beatriz: Muy amable, gracias.

ACTIVIDAD 7 - ¡ME ENCANTA EL FLAN!

Level 2 Textbook p. 284

TXT CD 6, Track 14

Escucha lo que dice Beatriz e indica si las oraciones son **ciertas** o **falsas**. Corrige las oraciones falsas.

Beatriz: En mi familia hay alguien famoso: mi tío, el chef Vicente. Si algún día tienes hambre y quieres comer algo sabrosísimo, ven a comer a su restaurante. Nadie cocina como mi tío: ni mi madre ni mi abuela. Tampoco yo... Y no hay ningún postre más rico que el flan que hace mi tío. Mmm... No hay nada mejor que esto...

TELEHISTORIA ESCENA 2

Level 2 Textbook p. 286

TXT CD 6, Track 15

Cliente: ¿Nadie trabaja aquí? ¿Cuál es la especialidad de la casa?

Beatriz: Ninguna. Pero las chuletas de cerdo están muy buenas.

Cliente: ¿Cómo las preparan?

Beatriz: Las preparan...o hervidas en caldo, o molidas y batidas con huevo. No. Perdón. Están crudas.

Cliente: ¿Y el filete también está crudo?

Beatriz: Lo preparan frito en aceite con algo...alguna verdura, creo.

Cliente: No me gusta ni el pollo asado ni el plato vegetariano. Me gustaría la paella.

Beatriz: ¡Excelente! ¿Y para beber? ¿Un refresco?

Cliente: No, gracias.

Beatriz: ¿Tal vez un té frío con limón?

Cliente: No, tampoco. Nada, gracias.

Beatriz: Muy bien. Perdone, ¿qué pidió?

Cliente: ¡La PAELLA!

PRONUNCIACIÓN

Level 2 Textbook p. 289

TXT CD 6, Track 16

Las letras **h**, **g** y **j**

We know that the Spanish **h** is silent. To form the sound that approximates the English **h**, Spanish uses the letter **g** (before **e** and **i**) or **j**. Listen and repeat.

h **h**ola **h**uevo zana**h**oria **h**ervido

g **G**erardo vegetariano pá**g**ina **g**imnasio

j **j**unio **j**ardín a**j**o mu**j**er

ACTIVIDAD 15 - ¡NO SE LO RECOMIENDO!

Level 2 Textbook p. 290

TXT CD 6, Track 17

Escucha la conversación y escribe lo que piden la chica y el chico.

Chica: ¿Nos recomienda la ensalada de verduras?

Camarera: No, señorita, no se la recomiendo. La lechuga no está muy fresca hoy. Pero el gazpacho está rico.

Chica: ¿Me lo trae, por favor? Y una hamburguesa con patatas fritas.

Camarera: Como no. ¿Y usted, señor?

Chico: No sé... ¿Cómo es el pollo a la mexicana?

Camarera: Es muy picante. ¿Se lo traigo?

Chico: Hmm, creo que no... ¿Hay algún plato vegetariano?

Camarera: Sí. Tenemos un sándwich de queso.

Chico: Hmmm... Sándwich de queso... sí, tráigamelo, por favor. Con verduras.

Camarera: Excelente. ¿Y para beber?

Chico: Para mí, nada, gracias.

Chica:¿Me trae un vaso de agua?

Camarera: Claro que sí, señorita. Se lo traigo ahora.

Chica: Muy amable.

TELEHISTORIA COMPLETA

Level 2 Textbook p. 291

TXT CD 6, Track 18

Escena 1 Resumen El tío Vicente les enseña a Beatriz y a José Luis a trabajar como camareros en su restaurante. Beatriz no lo escucha.

Escena 2 Resumen Beatriz empieza su nuevo trabajo, pero tiene problemas. Ella está muy desorganizada y hace muchos errores.

Escena 3

José Luis: Aquí están sus filetes. ¡Buen provecho!

Cliente 2: Necesito la cuenta. ¿Me la puede traer, por favor? Tengo prisa.

Cliente 3: Por favor, ¿me puede traer el flan? ¿Lo compartimos?

Cliente 4: Perdón. Gracias por atendernos. ¡Eres muy atento y un camarero excelente!

José Luis: Beatriz, ésta es la cuenta del señor de la mesa cinco. ¿Se la puedes dar? Y en la mesa dos quieren un flan. ¿Se lo puedes servir?

Beatriz: No quiero trabajar en un restaurante.

José Luis: Ni yo tampoco. Es un trabajo muy difícil.

Beatriz: ¿Qué podemos hacer? ¿Alguien te dio una buena propina?

José Luis: Sí... me la dieron unas señoras muy simpáticas de la mesa siete.

Beatriz: ¿Te podemos ayudar?

Audio Scripts

ACTIVIDAD 20 - INTEGRACIÓN

Level 2 Textbook p. 293

TXT CD 6, Track 19

Lee la crítica en una revista y otra en la radio. Compara los dos restaurantes, decide en cuál quieres cenar y recomiéndaselo a alguien.

INTEGRACIÓN, FUENTE 2

TXT CD 6, Track 20

Listen and take notes.

¿Es bello o feo el restaurante España Antigua?

¿Cómo es la comida?

¿Cuándo debes ir al restaurante? ¿Por qué?

Ana Gil: Hola, soy Ana Gil, aquí otra vez para hablar de los restaurantes de nuestra ciudad. ¿Usted ya probó el restaurante España Antigua? Si no, yo se lo recomiendo. El lugar es bellísimo, como un viejo palacio español, y la comida es sabrosísima. Si quiere alguna especialidad española, se la pueden servir. Pero no es barato. Comparta una paella con alguien si usted quiere comer bien pero no quiere pagar tanto. El servicio es un poco lento de jueves a sábado porque están ocupadísimos durante esos días. Haga una reservación o vaya otro día... ¡pero vaya!

LECTURA CULTURAL: DOS TRADICIONES CULINARIAS

Level 2 Textbook pp. 294–295

TXT CD 6, Track 21

El cocido madrileño es la comida más típica de Madrid. Este guiso es de garbanzos, diferentes verduras y carnes. Se hierve en agua y se sirve en tres platos separados, o vuelcos: la sopa, las verduras con los garbanzos, y la carne. Estos platos forman la base del típico menú madrileño. El mejor lugar para probar un menú madrileño es el restaurante Sobrino de Botín. Este restaurante se abrió en el año 1725. Está en un edificio del año 1590 y queda en un barrio histórico, en la calle de los Cuchilleros, cerca de la Plaza Mayor. Según el *Libro Guinness de los récords,* la Casa Botín, como también se conoce, es el restaurante más antiguo del mundo. En la Casa Botín sirven platos tradicionales de carne como el cochinillo asado y el cordero asado. Es un restaurante favorito de muchos españoles. Pero también muchos turistas lo visitan todos los días.

La carne, el pescado y los mariscos son los alimentos básicos de la región donde queda Montevideo. La parrillada (carne asada en una parrilla) es el plato de carne tradicional de la región. Como Montevideo queda en la costa, el pescado y los mariscos siempre están muy accesibles y son, por eso, los otros alimentos básicos. Un lugar muy especial para ir a comer parrilladas, pescado y mariscos en Montevideo es el Mercado del Puerto. El Mercado del Puerto se construyó en 1868. Es grande y muy bello: está hecho de metal, de piedra y de vidrio. Generalmente, la gente va al Mercado del Puerto para almorzar, no para cenar; muy pocos restaurantes están abiertos para la cena.

REPASO: ACTIVIDAD 1 - LISTEN AND UNDERSTAND

Level 2 Textbook p. 298

TXT CD 6, Track 22

Escucha lo que dice la camarera en un restaurante y escoge la respuesta lógica.

1. Bienvenidos. ¿Le puedo servir algo para beber?
2. Muy bien. ¿Y para comer? De entremés tenemos un gazpacho riquísimo y la especialidad de la casa es el pollo asado.
3. Aquí tiene el gazpacho. ¿Necesita algo más?
4. Permiso señor. Aquí tiene el pollo asado.
5. ¿Todo está bien?¿Le gustaría algo más?
6. De postre, ofrecemos una torta de chocolate. ¿Se la traigo?
7. Aquí tiene la cuenta. Muy buenas noches.

COMPARACIÓN CULTURAL: ¡QUÉ DELICIOSO!

Level 2 Textbook pp. 300–301

TXT CD 6, Track 23

Uruguay, Danilo

¡Saludos desde Montevideo! Yo me llamo Danilo. Me encanta comer asado con amigos en un buen restaurante. Es un plato simple pero sabroso de carne sazonada con sal, pimienta y vinagre. Después del asado, todos compartimos un mate, una bebida caliente de hierbas. ¡Buen provecho!

El Salvador, Juan

¡Hola! Me llamo Juan y soy de El Salvador. Aquí comemos muchas tortillas de maíz. A veces las comemos solas pero muchas veces las rellenamos con carne, frijoles y queso. Entonces se llaman pupusas. Las comemos con curtido, que es repollo, zanahoria y cebolla en vinagre salado. ¡Mmm, qué ricas!

España, Saskia

¡Qué tal! Soy Saskia y vivo en Valencia. Me parece que la comida más rica de España es la paella. Para hacerla, voy al mercado y compro ingredientes como pollo, tomate, arroz y muchos mariscos fresquísimos. Los domingos me gusta preparar una paella grande. La llevo a la playa y se la sirvo a toda mi familia. ¡Nos encanta!

REPASO INCLUSIVO: ACTIVIDAD 1 LISTEN, UNDERSTAND, AND COMPARE

Level 2 Textbook p. 304

TXT CD 6, Track 24

Listen to this conversation between a brother and sister in a supermarket in Spain and then answer the following questions.

Carmen: ¿Qué debemos servir en nuestra fiesta, Ignacio?

Ignacio: Debemos servir gazpacho, pollo asado, y ¡muchos postres!

Carmen: ¿Postres? No son muy saludables. ¿Qué piensas de una ensalada de espinaca?

Ignacio: ¿Espinaca? ¡Qué asco! Si tenemos que tener una ensalada, prefiero una ensalada de lechuga. Mira… esta lechuga aquí es fresquísima.

Carmen: Bueno, la podemos comprar. Pero quiero la espinaca también. Podemos mezclarlas en la ensalada.

Ignacio: Carmen, compra estos tomates y cebollas. Podemos ponerlos en la ensalada y también en el gazpacho.

Carmen: Buena idea. También necesitamos aceite y vinagre para la ensalada.

Ignacio: Están allí… pero, ¿dónde están las carnes?

Carmen: Están al otro lado del supermercado. ¿Necesitamos un pollo o dos?

Ignacio: Uno está bien…porque todos van a comer los postres riquísimos que voy a preparar. El flan, la tarta de chocolate, helado de fresa, helado de chocolate, helado de…

Carmen: ¡Ignacio! ¡¿Flan, helado, tarta?! ¡Uy! Pienso que unas frutas son buenas para el postre. Son muy saludables.

Ignacio: ¡Ay, por favor! ¿Frutas para el postre?

Carmen: Sí, quiero comprar uvas, manzanas y fresas.

Ignacio: Puedes comprarlas si yo puedo servir otros postres.

Carmen: Está bien. Podemos tener frutas, flan, y una tarta pequeña… ¡pero ningún helado! Ya tenemos demasiado.

WORKBOOK SCRIPTS WB CD 3

INTEGRACIÓN HABLAR

Level 2 Workbook p. 229

WB CD 3, Track 11

Escucha el mensaje telefónico que Nicolás le deja a Paula en su celular. Toma apuntes.

FUENTE 2

WB CD 3, Track 12

Nicolás: Hola, Paula. ¿Vamos a almorzar al restaurante Don Manolo? Yo sé que te encanta la comida allí. Hay comida para las personas que son vegetarianas, como tú. También hay comida para las personas que no son vegetarianas, como yo. Sabes que yo puedo comer platos vegetarianos o platos de carne. Después de cenar podemos ir a la heladería a comprar un helado o a la pastelería a comer un pastel.

Audio Scripts

INTEGRACIÓN ESCRIBIR

Level 2 Workbook p. 230

WB CD 3, Track 13

Escucha este anuncio para La Parrilla Deliciosa. Toma apuntes.

FUENTE 2

WB CD 3, Track 14

¡Buenos días, amigos! ¿Saben que hay un nuevo restaurante en el barrio? Se llama La Parrilla Deliciosa y ofrece todo tipo de carnes a la parrilla. Ustedes pueden probar chuletas de cerdo y filete a la parrilla. También preparan el pollo y las verduras a la parrilla. ¡Qué sabrosos! Llamen a sus amigos y vayan a La Parrilla Deliciosa. ¡Nos vemos allí!

ESCUCHAR A, ACTIVIDAD 1

Level 2 Workbook p. 231

WB CD 3, Track 15

Escucha la conversación de Verónica y el camarero. Luego, encierra en un círculo las comidas que pide Verónica.

Verónica: Buenos días, señor. Quiero comer algo muy rico. ¿Tiene el menú? ¿Puede traérmelo?

Camarero: Claro, con mucho gusto se lo traigo, señorita. Aquí está.

Verónica: ¿Cuál es la especialidad de la casa?

Camarero: Filete a la parrilla con ensalada de tomate y patatas asadas.

Verónica: ¡Delicioso! Sírvamelo, por favor. También quiero zumo de naranja y de postre, tarta de chocolate. Empiece con el filete.

Camarero: En un minuto se lo traigo.

ESCUCHAR A, ACTIVIDAD 2

Level 2 Workbook p. 231

WB CD 3, Track 16

Escucha la conversación entre Verónica y María, que hablan por teléfono. Luego, contesta las preguntas.

Verónica: ¿Hola? ¿María?¿Cómo estás?

María: Hola, Verónica. Estoy bien, ¿y tú? ¿Qué haces?

Verónica: Acabo de pedir la comida. Es deliciosa. Estoy comiendo un filete riquísimo.

María: Mmm, yo acabo de comer. Comí una chuleta de cerdo deliciosa. ¿Puedes llevarme al supermercado hoy?

Verónica: Sí, ¿qué tienes que comprar?

María: Voy a comprar algunas verduras frescas porque quiero preparar un gazpacho para cenar. ¡Te invito!

ESCUCHAR B, ACTIVIDAD 1

Level 2 Workbook p. 232

WB CD 3, Track 17

Escucha lo que dice Jaime. Lee cada oración y contesta cierto o falso.

Jaime: La paella es mi plato preferido. No hay nada como la paella, es riquísima. Mi mamá hace la paella más buena del mundo. Nadie la hace como ella. También hace un gazpacho muy rico. Mezcla muchos tomates frescos y molidos con ajo. Así hace esta sopa fría. Siempre hay algún invitado a comer y nunca sale con hambre. Tampoco sale sin pedirle la receta a mi mamá, pero ella nunca se la da.

ESCUCHAR B, ACTIVIDAD 2

Level 2 Workbook p. 232

WB CD 3, Track 18

Escucha la conversación de Antonio y Maribel. Luego, contesta las preguntas con oraciones completas.

Antonio: Maribel, ¿le das a mamá la receta de Laura?

Maribel: Sí, Antonio. Tranquilo, yo se la doy. ¿De qué es la receta?

Antonio: Es de unas patatas hervidas que son deliciosas. No hay nada tan rico como esas patatas.

Maribel: ¿Y qué las hace tan especiales?

Antonio: Creo que el secreto está en el vinagre que se le añade al agua. Y después, cuando están en el plato, se les pone pimienta.

Maribel: ¡Qué asco! No me gustan las comidas picantes.

ESCUCHAR C, ACTIVIDAD 1

Level 2 Workbook p. 233

WB CD 3, Track 19

Escucha la conversación entre Elena y Elisa, la madre de su amiga. Toma apuntes. Luego, completa las siguientes oraciones.

Elena: Señora, su hija dice que usted quiere la receta de mi súper sándwich.

Elsa: Sí, Elena. ¿Puedes dármela?

Elena: Claro. Corte el pan. Compre jamón, queso, lechuga y tomate. Tome el jamón y el tomate y póngalos primero. Luego, tome el queso y la lechuga y póngalos encima.

Elsa: Parece delicioso.

Elena: Sí, lo es. Y al final, añada mayonesa. Es mejor comerlo caliente.

Elsa: ¡Sabroso!

ESCUCHAR C, ACTIVIDAD 2

Level 2 Workbook p. 233

WB CD 3, Track 20

Escucha lo que dice Carina. Toma apuntes. Luego, contesta las preguntas con oraciones completas.

Carina: Soy Carina y soy vegetariana. No como nada de carne. Nadie me entiende, pero creo que está mal comer animales. Por eso, siempre como frijoles, verduras, huevos, leche y algunas otras comidas que no llevan carne. Los espaguetis me gustan con tomate, pero sin carne. No se la pongo. Mi sopa preferida es una de verduras cortadas muy pequeñas y hervidas poco tiempo en un caldo de cebolla. Están casi crudas. Se la doy a mis amigos pero a ninguno le gusta.

ASSESSMENT SCRIPTS

LESSON 2 TEST: ESCUCHAR

ACTIVIDAD A

Modified Assessment Book p. 182

On-level Assessment Book p. 238

Pre-AP Assessment Book p. 182

TEST CD 2, Track 3

Escucha el siguiente audio. Luego, completa la actividad A.

Sue es una amiga de Paqui y Álvaro de Estados Unidos. Ella acaba de llegar a Madrid. Es su primer viaje a España y quiere practicar su español en un restaurante típico. Está pensando en comer una de esas comidas españolas de que tanto hablaron sus profesores en las clases de español. Sue entra en el primer restaurante que ve llamado Como en tu Casa porque debajo del nombre del restaurante dice "Especialidades para los Turistas." El camarero sienta a Sue en una mesa.

Camarero: Buenas tardes, señorita. ¿Qué va a pedir de almuerzo?

Sue: ¿Cuáles son las especialidades para los turistas?

Camarero: Hamburguesas, patatas fritas, pizza…

Sue: Pero… yo vine de Virginia, muy lejos de aquí, para comer platos típicos españoles: paella, gazpacho… no hamburguesas.

Camarero: Disculpe, señorita, pero ésas son las comidas que normalmente les gustan a los norteamericanos. Por eso decimos "Especialidades para los turistas."

Sue: Bien, tráigame una hamburguesa con papas fritas.

ACTIVIDAD B

TEST CD 2, Track 4

Escucha el siguiente audio. Luego, completa la actividad B.

Después de no tener suerte ayer en el restaurante Como en tu Casa, esta noche Paqui y Álvaro decidieron invitar a Sue a un restaurante típico español, que se llamaba Las Cuevas de Luis Candela.

Camarero: Buenas noches. Aquí tenéis el menú.

Álvaro: Sue, ¿qué vas a pedir? Te recomiendo la paella. Es buenísima aquí.

Sue: Buena idea. ¿Nos puede traer la paella para tres?

Camarero: Sí, claro. ¿Quieren un entremés?

Álvaro: No, gracias.

Camarero: ¿Y para beber?

Álvaro: Té frío para los tres.

Camarero: ¿Y de postre?

Sue: Yo quiero flan. ¿Y vosotros?

Álvaro: Tráigame la tarta de chocolate.

Paqui: A mí también, por favor.

Camarero: ¡Excelente! ¡Buen provecho!

UNIT 5 TEST: ESCUCHAR ACTIVIDAD A

Modified Assessment Book p. 194

On-level Assessment Book p. 250

Pre-AP Assessment Book p. 194

TEST CD 2, Track 5

Pepe Machado: Bienvenidos, mis queridos amigos. Ustedes me han llamado muchas veces para pedir una receta de patatas. Hoy se las voy a dar. Tomen lápiz y papel, que ya vamos a empezar.

Esta receta es para tres personas y éstos son los ingredientes:

4 huevos

3 patatas

1 cebolla

aceite (1/4 litro)

sal

pimienta

Primero deben lavar las patatas y cortarlas. También corten la cebolla. Frían las patatas y la cebolla y mezclen todo bien. Batan los huevos con la sal y añádanlos a las patatas y cebolla. Cocine bien estos ingredientes, de un lado y después del otro. Pueden comer la comida caliente o fría, como plato vegetariano o al lado del plato principal. ¡Buen provecho!

ACTIVIDAD B

Modified Assessment Book p. 194

On-level Assessment Book p. 250

Pre-AP Assessment Book p. 194

TEST CD 2, Track 6

Escucha el siguiente audio. Luego, completa la actividad B.

Camarero: Buenas noches, y bienvenidos a nuestro restaurante, que se llama La madrileña. Mi nombre es Esteban. Quiero decirles cuáles son las especialidades de la casa esta noche. De entremés tenemos caldo de pollo y gazpacho. De platos principales tenemos chuletas de cerdo muy sabrosas; filete a la parrilla con papas fritas; y nuestro plato de carne madrileño. La ensalada César es una de nuestras especialidades también, servida con pan fresco. Nuestros postres son los mejores de Madrid. El flan y la tarta de chocolate les van a encantar con nuestro café. ¿Qué les puedo traer?

HERITAGE LEARNER SCRIPTS HL CDs 2 & 5

INTEGRACIÓN HABLAR

Level 2 HL Workbook p. 231

HL CD 2, Track 5

Escucha el mensaje que dejó el señor José Miguel Domínguez en el contestador de su esposa Concepción. Puedes tomar notas mientras escuchas y luego completa la actividad.

FUENTE 2

HL CD 2, Track 6

Concepción, soy yo. ¿Dónde estás? Ah, mujer, te llamo sólo porque quiero descargar la mala energía. Es que acabo de comer en el restaurante de tu primo Carlos y él no estaba allí. Mira que el servicio fue pésimo. Nunca me trataron tan mal en un restaurante. El camarero hablaba constantemente con su novia por teléfono y me trajo a la mesa la comida equivocada, unas patatas fritas fatales. Yo le pedí un bocadillo de chorizo. Mira, mujer, háblale a Carlos y cuéntale, que al ojo del amo engorda el caballo… Bueno, regreso a la oficina, adiós.

INTEGRACIÓN ESCRIBIR

Level 2 HL Workbook p. 232

HL CD 2, Track 7

Escucha un anuncio de radio de otro restaurante en Madrid. Puedes tomar notas mientras escuchas y luego completa la actividad.

FUENTE 2

HL CD 2, Track 8

Desde la próxima semana, Restaurantes El Gitano anuncia su nueva plaza a un costado de la Biblioteca Nacional, sobre el Paseo de Recoletos. Los bocadillos de su predilección, siempre imitados, jamás igualados. Usted conoce nuestro prestigio, usted conoce nuestro servicio. Nuestra carta le ofrece entradas como el chorizo criollo, croquetas caseras de jamón o morcilla; ensaladas de queso de cabra y espinacas; carnes principales como escalope milanesa, chuletas de cordero, entrecot a la parrilla. Especial de inauguración: Comida de tres cursos 34 . ¡Lo esperamos!

LESSON 2 TEST: ESCUCHAR ACTIVIDAD A

HL Assessment Book p. 188

HL CD 4, Track 3

Marta y Andrés están en el nuevo restaurante de su localidad. Después de escucharlos, contesta las siguientes preguntas usando oraciones completas.

Andrés: ¿Qué te parece el sitio? Lo abrieron hace pocas semanas.

Marta: Se ve muy bien. Me gusta la decoración. ¿Cuál es la especialidad de la casa?

Andrés: Carlos me dijo que preparan comida española y que se especializan en paellas.

Camarero: Buenas noches, señores. ¿En qué puedo servirles?

Andrés: ¿Puede traernos el menú, por favor?

Camarero: Con mucho gusto. ¿Desean tomar algo mientras deciden?

Andrés: ¿Me puede traer un jugo de frutas tropicales?

Camarero: Y usted, señora, ¿desea tomar algo?

Marta: Sí, tráigame un vaso de agua, por favor.

Camarero: En seguida. ¿Puedo hacerles una recomendación?

Andrés: Por supuesto. Es muy atento.

Camarero: La paella valenciana es nuestra especialidad. Se la recomiendo.

Andrés: Nos han hablado de ese plato. También un amigo nos lo recomendó.

Camarero: También les puedo ofrecer una deliciosa chuleta de cerdo a la parrilla, un filete de bacalao en salsa verde, un pollo hervido en caldo de vegetales…

Marta: Yo quisiera probar esa paella.

Andrés: Pediremos la paella.

Camarero: ¿Desea acompañarla con alguna otra cosa?

Andrés: Una ensalada de lechugas variadas estará bien.

Camarero: Excelente. Se la traigo en seguida.

Marta: Gracias por atendernos.

Camarero: Es un placer. ¡Buen provecho!

ACTIVIDAD B

HL Assessment Book p. 188

HL CD 4, Track 4

Félix y Silvia van a merendar en el lugar de siempre, pero hoy ocurre algo inesperado. Escúchalos y luego completa las oraciones que faltan.

Félix: Oiga, pero esto no es lo que pedimos.

Silvia: Sí, yo no pedí esto. No me gusta el té.

Camarero: ¿Cómo? ¿No le gusta? Pero usted lo pidió.

Silvia: No. Yo pedí un helado de vainilla.

Félix: Y a mí déme la torta de chocolate que le pedí.

Camarero: Le aseguro que este batido de plátano es muy bueno.

Félix: No lo dudo, pero no es lo que yo pedí.

Camarero: Entonces, ¿qué pidió? Dígamelo.

Félix: Pedí lo de siempre, la torta de chocolate.

Camarero: Por favor… disculpen. Creo que estoy enamorado.

Silvia: Entonces lo disculpamos. A todos nos puede pasar.

Félix: Pero ahora tráiganos lo que pedimos.

Audio Scripts

UNIT 5 TEST: ESCUCHAR, ACTIVIDAD A

HL Assessment Book p. 200

HL CD 4, Track 5

Escucha la siguiente conversación imaginaria entre don Quijote y su Sancho Panza. Responde las siguientes preguntas con oraciones completas.

Don Quijote: Mi buen Sancho, hace ya más de tres horas que el sol brilla en lo alto y aún no hemos comido nada.

Sancho Panza: Mi señor, entienda que me faltan unos pocos ingredientes para terminar la sopa.

Don Quijote: ¿Y cuáles son? ¿Es tan necesario ponerlos?

Sancho Panza: Sí, porque sin ellos no tendrá el gusto delicadísimo que a usted tanto le gusta.

Don Quijote: Muy bien. ¡Busquémoslos! Por aquí ha de haber algún sembradío.

Sancho Panza: Necesitamos cebollas, ajos, pimienta, unos pocos limones y algo del dorado aceite de oliva.

Don Quijote: El aceite se lo pedimos a alguien…aunque podemos hacerlo si conseguimos aceitunas para prensar.

Sancho Panza: Mire, señor por allá, cientos de árboles cargadísimos de limones y aceitunas!

Don Quijote: ¡Adelante, Sancho! ¡Avancemos! ¡Tomemos los frutos que la tierra nos ofrece!

Sancho Panza: Señor, ¿y si aparecen los dueños? ¿Qué hacemos?

Don Quijote: ¡Pues los invitamos a comer con nosotros! ¿Es que acaso pensabas algo diferente?

Sancho Panza: No, que no; tiene usted razón. ¿Y si no nos alcanza con lo que hay preparado?

Don Quijote: Que si va a alcanzar, Sancho, no te preocupes. ¿Qué no ves que un pollo con sopa es más que suficiente para alimentarnos? Además que hemos de tener algunas naranjas e higos en el zurrón.

Sancho Panza: Que no, que los higos se acabaron y de las naranjas ya no queda ninguna.

Don Quijote: Encontraremos más. Siempre hay algo más dentro del zurrón, ¿algunos dátiles? ¿Algo de miel?

Sancho Panza: Sí, señor, nos quedan algo de dátiles y algo de miel también.

Don Quijote: Entonces, no perdamos más tiempo, mi fiel amigo; que esa riquísima sopa que estás preparando está casi lista y el pan se quema sobre el brasero!

ACTIVIDAD B

HL Assessment Book p. 200

HL CD 4, Track 6

Escribe las oraciones que vas a escuchar a continuación. Luego ordénalas según la secuencia que corresponda.

1. Revuelva la mezcla mientras hierve el chocolate.
2. Agregue un palito de canela y tres clavos de olor.
3. Revuelva a fuego medio hasta que el chocolate espese.
4. En una olla, coloque leche, azúcar y una tableta de chocolate.
5. Retire del fuego y deje reposar antes de servir.
6. Deje hervir el chocolate unos minutos y baje el fuego.

Nombre ____________ Clase ____________ Fecha ____________

Map/Culture Activities *España*

❶ Al oeste de España hay otro país en la península Ibérica. ¿Cómo se llama? También hay otro país en la península que está entre España y Francia. ¿Cuál es? Localízalos y escribe sus nombres en el mapa.

❷ Al oeste de España esta el Océano Atlántico y al este está el Mar Mediterráneo. En cada uno hay un grupo de islas. Localízalos y escribe sus nombres en el mapa.

❸ Ahora localiza estas ciudades en el mapa y escribe sus nombres. También escribe los nombres de las ciudades autónomas que pertenecen (*belong*) a España, pero están en Marruecos.

1. Barcelona
2. Granada
3. Sevilla
4. Toledo
5. Valencia
6. Ceuta
7. Melilla

Map/Culture Activities *España*

❹ Usa la información de tu libro para elegir la respuesta correcta que completa las frases de abajo.

1. Antonio Banderas y Penélope Cruz probablemente trabajarían con _____ .
   a. Pablo Picasso **b.** Carmen Lafloret **c.** Pedro Almodóvar
2. Antonio Gaudí fue un arquitecto que diseñó (*designed*) edificios _____ .
   a. modernos **b.** clásicos **c.** góticos
3. En España hablan _____ idiomas diferentes.
   a. dos **b.** cuatro **c.** seis
4. El Greco nacío en _____ .
   a. Grecia **b.** Francia **c.** España

❺ El artista conocido como El Greco vivió en Toledo durante muchos años y por lo tanto (*therefore*) él siempre está relacionado con esa ciudad. ¿Hay artistas relacionados con la región donde tú vives? ¿Qué tipo de artista es?

____

____

____

Nombre ______________________ Clase ______________ Fecha ______________

Map/Culture Activities Answer Key

ESPAÑA

Page 83

❶ *Refer to map above.*

❷ *Refer to map above.*

❸ *Refer to map above.*

Page 84

❹

1. c
2. a
3. b
4. a

❺ *Answers will vary.*

Fine Art Activities

Naturaleza muerta, Àngel Planells

Àngel Planells was born in Cadaqués, a town in the Cataluña region of Spain, in 1901. When he was sixteen, he moved to Barcelona to study lithography and drawing, and it was there that he met painter Salvador Dalí. Through the years, he met and studied with many well-known artists, and eventually became a painter himself. Although he shifted to commercial art forms, Planells is best known for his work in surrealism.

Naturaleza muerta is one of Àngel Planells's early works.

1a. List those food items featured in the work that are familiar to you on the lines below.

____

____

b. Explain what meal of the day you think this is and why.

____

____

2. Describe the ways in which Planells creates a realistic sense of dimension in *Naturaleza muerta*. Be specific in your answer.

____

____

____

____

____

Still Life (ca. 1925), Àngel Planells i Cruanyes. Oil on canvas. Collection J.B. Cendros, Barcelona. The Bridgeman Art Library.

Fine Art Activities

La vendimia, Francisco Goya
El 3 de Mayo de 1808 en Madrid, Francisco Goya

Famed Spanish painter Francisco Goya's artistic career spanned over 60 years. Goya's personal changes and his reaction to the political events of his time had a dramatic effect on the evolution of his work. His early paintings focused primarily on religious subjects and depictions of everyday life. Eventually he became the court painter of King Charles IV, for whom he created numerous paintings and portraits in the carefree rococo style popular at the time. Decreasing physical and emotional health led him to explore darker subjects and colors as his paintings became less accepted by the public. Finally, a violent war with France added a certain brutality to his work, and he began a series of "Black Paintings," which often contain gruesome, dark and terrifying images.

Compare and contrast the works *La vendimia,* painted in 1787, and *El 3 de Mayo de 1808 en Madrid,* painted in 1814, by Francisco Goya.

1. Study the style of each painting carefully. Look at the colors used, the layout of the scenes, the attention to detail and the visual realism. What differences do you see? Are there any similarities? Compare and contrast the style of *La vendimia* with that of *El 3 de Mayo*.

____

____

____

____

2. Describe your impressions of the two paintings. Which do you think is a better work of art? Why? Justify your answer by referring to specific aspects of the painting you prefer.

____

____

____

____

Autumn, or *The Grape Harvest* (1786-87), Francisco José de Goya y Lucientes. Oil on canvas. Prado, Madrid, Spain. Giraudon/The Bridgeman Art Library.

The Third of May, 1808 (1814), Francisco de Goya y Lucientes. 266 cm x 345 cm, oil on canvas. Erich Lessing/Art Resource, NY.

Fine Art Activities

La niña con pasteles, María Blanchard

María Blanchard was a Spanish artist best known for her cubist works. Cubist artists often use a limited color palette and focus on shapes and lines rather than on realism. Works in this style can be simple or complex, completely abstract or largely recognizable. *La niña con pasteles* reflects Blanchard's eventual shift from strict cubism to figuratively realistic works.

Complete the following activities based on your interpretation of María Blanchard's *La niña con pasteles*.

1. Blanchard's early works are highly abstract, while her later works are almost instantly familiar. Describe those elements of *La niña con pasteles* that reflect Blanchard's cubist foundation.

____

____

____

____

____

____

2. What is the mood of this painting? How do you think Blanchard wants you to feel about the painting and its subject? Use examples from the work to clarify your answer.

____

____

____

____

____

____

____

L'enfant aux pâtisseries (*Child with Cakes*) (1921), María Blanchard. Oil on canvas. Musée National d'Art Moderne, Centre Pompidou, Paris/The Bridgeman Art Library.

Fine Art Activities

Retrato de Felipe II, Sofonisba Anguisciola

Sofonisba Anguisciola was a rarity during her time. She was born in Italy in 1535, during an age when women seldom were encouraged to pursue their talents outside the home. With her father's support, Anguisciola gained recognition as an artist and eventually worked as the official court painter of Philip II of Spain.

Study *Retrato de Felipe II*, by Sofonisba Anguisciola, and complete the following activities.

1. What does the artist tell us about her subject? Observe the clothing, posture and simple possessions of the king. Explain what you think Felipe II was like based on the artist's rendition.

____

____

____

____

____

____

2. If you were commissioned to paint a current figure of importance, whom would you choose? What elements would you include in your portrait to show your subject's personality and significance? Choose the subject of your portrait and explain what your work would look like.

____

____

____

____

____

____

____

Philip II of Spain (1565), Sofonisba Anguisciola. Oil on canvas. Prado, Madrid, Spain/The Bridgeman Art Library.

Fine Art Activities Answer Key

***NATURALEZA MUERTA,* ÀNGEL PLANELLS, page 86**

1a. apple, juice, artichokes, bread, eggs, walnuts, leeks/onions, peach/apricot

b. *Answers will vary.*

2. *Answers will vary.* Students should focus on the artist's use of light and shadow (fruit peel, bread, nuts, towel), reflection (glass and knife) and perspective.

LA VENDIMIA, FRANCISCO GOYA

***EL 3 DE MAYO DE 1808 EN MADRID,* FRANCISCO GOYA, page 87**

1. *Answers will vary.* Students should be able to contrast the delicacy and balance of the first with the roughness and chaos of the second.

2. *Answers will vary.* Students should be able to explain their answers specifically.

***LA NIÑA CON PASTELES,* MARÍA BLANCHARD, page 88**

1. *Answers will vary.* Students may focus on the geometric shadowing on the tablecloth, the shape-focus in the painting, the muted colors, perspective, etc.

2. *Answers will vary.*

***RETRATO DE FELIPE II,* SOFONISBA ANGUISCIOLA, page 89**

1. *Answers will vary.* Students may note his austere expression, unadorned clothing, or the rosary in his hand as indicators of his personality.

2. *Answers will vary.*

Date: ________________

Dear Family:

We are about to begin *Unidad 5* of the Level 2 *¡Avancemos!* program. It focuses on authentic culture and real-life communication using Spanish in Spain. It practices reading, writing, listening, and speaking, and introduces students to culture typical of Spain.

Through completing the activities, students will employ critical thinking skills as they compare the Spanish language and the culture of Spain with their own community. They will also connect to other academic subjects, using their knowledge of Spanish to access new information. In this unit, students are learning to identify and describe ingredients, talk about food preparation and follow recipes, give instructions and make recommendations, order meals in a restaurant, talk about meals and dishes, and describe food and service. They are also learning about grammar—adjectives ending in **-ísimo, usted/ ustedes** commands, pronoun placement with commands, affirmative and negative words, and double object pronouns.

Please feel free to call me with any questions or concerns you might have as your student practices reading, writing, listening, and speaking in Spanish.

Sincerely,

Nombre ______________________ Clase ______________ Fecha ______________

Family Involvement Activity

STEP 1
Prepare a variety of food samples. You may use the suggestions from the table below or you may create your own dishes. Try to incorporate some Hispanic flavors in your food samples.

STEP 2
Invite your family to sit at a table. Blindfold all participants and provide them each with a spoon and several small slips of paper. Have each participant sample the first dish.

STEP 3
Without speaking, participants should remove their blindfolds and write down the flavors they tasted and the ingredients they think the dish contains.

STEP 4
Collect the slips of paper and read the answers aloud. Use the table below to record the names of participants and place a check mark next to the foods they correctly identified.

STEP 5
Repeat steps 2–5 until all dishes have been sampled.

Participant names

Foods sampled

Grated carrots with lemon juice

Chopped apples and pears

Popcorn with salt and chili powder

Flan

Who has the best sense of taste? ______________________________

Absent Student Copymasters

Presentación / Práctica de vocabulario

Materials Checklist

- ☐ Student text
- ☐ DVD 2
- ☐ Video Activities Copymasters, pages 49 and 50
- ☐ *Cuaderno,* pages 197–199
- ☐ *Cuaderno para hispanohablantes,* pages 197–200
- ☐ TXT CD 6 Tracks 1–2
- ☐ Did You Get It? Copymasters, pages 1 and 3
- ☐ ClassZone.com

Steps to Follow

- ☐ Study the vocabulary of **Presentación de vocabulario** (pp. 254–255) by looking at the photos and reading the words and accompanying text. Watch the DVD and complete the Video Activities Copymasters.
- ☐ Practice the words in the **Más vocabulario** box on page 255. Read the words aloud. Write the words in your notebook.
- ☐ Do **Práctica de vocabulario** (p. 256). Complete **Actividades 1, 2,** and **3**.
- ☐ Complete *Cuaderno,* pages pages 197, 198, and 199.
  OR
  Complete *Cuaderno para hispanohablantes,* pages 197, 198, 199, and 200.
- ☐ Check your comprehension by completing the **Para y piensa** box on page 256.
- ☐ Complete the Did You Get It? Copymasters, pages 1 and 3.

If You Don't Understand...

- ☐ Watch the DVD in a quiet place. If you get lost, stop the DVD and replay the segment.
- ☐ Listen to the CD as many times as necessary.
- ☐ Review the activity directions and study the model. Try to follow the model in your own answers.
- ☐ If you need a partner to complete the activity, practice both parts.
- ☐ Use the Interactive Flashcards to help you study the lesson.
- ☐ Think about what you are trying to say when you write a sentence. After you write your sentence, check to make sure that it says what you wanted to say.

Absent Student Copymasters

Level 2 pp. 257–258

Vocabulario en contexto

Materials Checklist

- ☐ Student text
- ☐ DVD 2
- ☐ Video Activities Copymasters, pages 51 and 52
- ☐ TXT CD 6 Track 3
- ☐ Did You Get It? Copymasters, pages 2 and 3

Steps to Follow

- ☐ Look at the photos on page 257. What do you think is happening?
- ☐ Read **Cuando lees** and **Cuando escuchas** under *Strategies* (p. 257). Copy the questions.
- ☐ Try to answer the questions in **Cuando lees** before watching the DVD.
- ☐ Watch DVD 2 without your book. Then watch the DVD again and complete the Video Activities Copymasters.
- ☐ Look at the dialogue in the book. Follow along in the book as you watch and listen to the DVD. Use the pictures and context to help you understand the dialogue.
- ☐ Complete **Actividades 4** and **5** on page 258.
- ☐ Check your comprehension by completing the **Para y piensa** box on page 258.
- ☐ Complete the Did You Get It? Copymasters, pages 2 and 3.

If You Don't Understand...

- ☐ Make sure you are in an area where you can concentrate.
- ☐ Read the activity directions again. Write the directions in your own words.
- ☐ Read the model before starting so you know what to do. Copy the model.
- ☐ Say what you want to write before you write it.
- ☐ If you have any questions, write them down so you can ask your teacher later.
- ☐ Practice both parts of any partner activities.
- ☐ Read your answers aloud to make sure they say what you wanted to say.

Nombre ______________________ Clase ______________ Fecha ______________

Absent Student Copymasters

Level 2 pp. 259–261

Presentación / Práctica de gramática

Materials Checklist

- ☐ Student text
- ☐ *Cuaderno,* pages 200–202
- ☐ *Cuaderno para hispanohablantes,* pages 201–203
- ☐ TXT CD 6 Tracks 4–5
- ☐ Did You Get It? Copymasters, pages 4 and 5
- ☐ ClassZone.com

Steps to Follow

- ☐ Study **usted/ustedes** commands (p. 259).
- ☐ Do **Actividades 6**, **7**, **8**, and **9** (pp. 260–261). Use TXT CD 6 Track 4 to complete **Actividad 7.**
- ☐ Listen to the **Pronunciación** section of TXT CD 6 Track 5. Pronounce the words aloud.
- ☐ Complete *Cuaderno,* pages 200, 201, and 202.
  OR
  Complete *Cuaderno para hispanohablantes,* pages 201, 202, and 203.
- ☐ Check your comprehension by completing the **Para y piensa** box on page 261.
- ☐ Complete the Did You Get It? Copymasters, pages 4 and 5.

If You Don't Understand...

- ☐ Do the activities that you understand first.
- ☐ For activities that require listening, listen to the CD in a quiet place. If you get lost, stop the CD and go back.
- ☐ Write the model on your paper. Try to follow the model in your own answers.
- ☐ Read aloud everything that you write. Be sure that you understand what you are reading.
- ☐ Write down any questions you have for your teacher.
- ☐ If the activity has parts for two people, practice both parts.
- ☐ Think about what you are trying to say when you write a sentence. After you write your sentence, check to make sure that it says what you wanted to say.
- ☐ Use the Animated Grammar to help you understand.
- ☐ Use the Leveled Grammar Practice on the @Home Tutor.

Absent Student Copymasters

Level 2 pp. 262–263

Gramática en contexto

Materials Checklist

- ☐ Student text
- ☐ Video Activities Copymasters, pages 53 and 54
- ☐ DVD 2
- ☐ TXT CD 6 Track 6
- ☐ Did You Get It? Copymasters, pages 4, 6, and 10

Steps to Follow

- ☐ Look at the photos on page 262. What do you think is happening?
- ☐ Read **Cuando lees** and **Cuando escuchas** under *Strategies* (p. 262). Copy the questions.
- ☐ Read the script and try to understand the dialogue based on the pictures. Try to answer the questions in **Cuando lees.**
- ☐ Watch DVD 2 without your book. Then watch the DVD again and complete the Video Activities Copymasters.
- ☐ Look at the dialogue in the book. Follow along in the book as you watch and listen to the DVD. Use the pictures and context to help you understand the dialogue.
- ☐ Study the words in the **También se dice** box.
- ☐ Complete **Actividades 10**, **11**, and **12** on page 263.
- ☐ Check your comprehension by completing the **Para y piensa** box on page 263.
- ☐ Complete the Did You Get It? Copymasters, pages 4, 6, and 10.

If You Don't Understand...

- ☐ Use the images to help you understand the DVD.
- ☐ Listen to the CD as many times as necessary.
- ☐ Reread the activity directions. Write the directions in your own words.
- ☐ Read the model a few times so you are certain that you understand what to do. Follow the model.
- ☐ If you have any questions, write them down for your teacher to answer later.
- ☐ Practice both parts of any partner activities.
- ☐ After you write a sentence, check to make sure that it says what you wanted to say.

Absent Student Copymasters

Level 2 pp. 264–266

Presentación / Práctica de gramática

Materials Checklist

- ☐ Student text
- ☐ *Cuaderno,* pages 203–205
- ☐ *Cuaderno para hispanohablantes,* pages 204–207
- ☐ TXT CD 6 Track 6
- ☐ Did You Get It? Copymasters, pages 7, 8, and 11
- ☐ ClassZone.com

Steps to Follow

- ☐ Study pronoun placement with commands (p. 264).
- ☐ Do **Actividades 13**, **14**, and **15** (pp. 265–266).
- ☐ Complete *Cuaderno,* pages 203, 204, and 205.
  OR
  Complete *Cuaderno para hispanohablantes,* pages 204, 205, 206, and 207.
- ☐ Check your comprehension by completing the **Para y piensa** box on page 266.
- ☐ Complete the Did You Get It? Copymasters, pages 7, 8, and 11.

If You Don't Understand…

- ☐ If you are having trouble with an activity, complete the ones you can do first.
- ☐ Listen to the CD as many times as you need to complete the activity.
- ☐ Review the activity directions and study the model. Try to follow the model in your own answers.
- ☐ Write down any questions you have for your teacher.
- ☐ If the activity has parts for two people, practice both parts.
- ☐ Use the Animated Grammar to help you understand.
- ☐ Use the Leveled Grammar Practice on the @Home Tutor.

Absent Student Copymasters

Level 2 pp. 267–269

Todo junto

Materials Checklist

- ☐ Student Text
- ☐ DVD 2
- ☐ Video Activities Copymasters, pages 55 and 56
- ☐ *Cuaderno,* pages 206–207
- ☐ *Cuaderno para hispanohablantes,* pages 208–209
- ☐ TXT CD 6 Tracks 7–9
- ☐ Did You Get It? Copymasters, pages 7 and 9
- ☐ WB CD 3 Tracks 1–4
- ☐ HL CD 2 Tracks 1–4

Steps to Follow

- ☐ Look at the photos on page 267. What do you think is happening?
- ☐ Read **Cuando lees** and **Cuando escuchas** under *Strategies* (p. 267). Copy the questions.
- ☐ Review the content of DVD 2.
- ☐ Read the script and try to understand the dialogue based on the picture. Try to answer the questions in **Cuando lees.**
- ☐ Watch DVD 2 without your book. Then watch the DVD again and complete the Video Activities Copymasters.
- ☐ Look at the dialogue in the book. Follow along as you watch and listen to the DVD. Use the pictures and context to help you understand the dialogue.
- ☐ Complete **Actividades 17, 18, 19, 20**, and **21** on pages 268 and 269. Use TXT CD 6 Tracks 8–9 with **Actividad 20.**
- ☐ Complete *Cuaderno,* pages 206 and 207.
  OR
  Complete *Cuaderno para hispanohablantes,* pages 208 and 209.
- ☐ Check your comprehension by completing the **Para y piensa** box on page 269.
- ☐ Complete the Did You Get It? Copymasters, pages 7 and 9.

Absent Student Copymasters

Level 2 pp. 270–272

Lectura y Conexiones

Materials Checklist

- [ ] Student text
- [ ] TXT CD 6 Track 10

Steps to Follow

- [ ] Read and complete *Strategy:* **Leer** (p. 270).
- [ ] Read **Dos odas de Pablo Neruda** on pages 270 and 271. Complete the chart from *Strategy:* **Leer**.
- [ ] Look at the photos and reread the odes.
- [ ] Follow along with the text on TXT CD 6 Track 10.
- [ ] Check your comprehension by completing the **¿Comprendiste?** and **¿Y tú?** sections of **Para y piensa** box on page 271.
- [ ] Read **Las comunidades autónomas** on pages 272.
- [ ] Describe a healthy dish in **Proyecto 1, La salud**.
- [ ] Create a timeline as directed in **Proyecto 2, La Historia**.
- [ ] Try to find a recording of Spanish music to complete **La música** in **Proyecto 3.**

If You Don't Understand…

- [ ] Listen to the CD in a quiet place. Play the CD as many times as you need.
- [ ] Read the activity directions again. Write the directions in your own words.
- [ ] Read everything aloud. Be sure that you understand what you are reading.
- [ ] If you have any questions, write them down so you can ask your teacher later.
- [ ] Think about what you are trying to say when you write a sentence. After you write your sentence, check to make sure that it says what you wanted to say.

Absent Student Copymasters

Level 2 **pp. 274–275**

Repaso de la lección

Materials Checklist

- ☐ Student text
- ☐ *Cuaderno,* pages 208–219
- ☐ *Cuaderno para hispanohablantes,* pages 210–219
- ☐ TXT CD 6 Track 10
- ☐ WB CD 3 Tracks 5–10

Steps to Follow

- ☐ Read the bullet points under **¡Llegada!** on page 274.
- ☐ Complete **Actividades 1**, **2**, **3**, **4**, and **5** (pp. 274–275). Listen to TXT CD 6 Track 10 to complete **Actividad 1.**
- ☐ Complete *Cuaderno,* pages 208, 209, and 210.
- ☐ Complete *Cuaderno,* pages 211, 212, and 213.
  OR
  Complete *Cuaderno para hispanohablantes,* pages 210, 211, and 212–213.
- ☐ Complete *Cuaderno,* pages 214, 215, and 216.
  OR
  Complete *Cuaderno para hispanohablantes,* pages 214, 215, and 216.
- ☐ Complete *Cuaderno,* pages 217, 218, and 219.
  OR
  Complete *Cuaderno para hispanohablantes,* pages 217, 218, and 219.

If You Don't Understand...

- ☐ If you are having trouble with an activity, complete the ones you can do first.
- ☐ For activities that require the CD, listen to the CD in a quiet place. If you get lost, stop the CD and go back.
- ☐ Review the activity directions and study the model. Try to follow the model in your own answers.
- ☐ Write down any questions you have for your teacher.

Absent Student Copymasters

Level 2 pp. 278–280

Presentación / Práctica de vocabulario

Materials Checklist

- ☐ Student text
- ☐ DVD 2
- ☐ Video Activities Copymasters, pages 57 and 58
- ☐ *Cuaderno,* pages 220–222
- ☐ *Cuaderno para hispanohablantes,* pages 220–223
- ☐ TXT CD 6 Tracks 11–12
- ☐ Did You Get It? Copymasters, pages 12 and 13
- ☐ ClassZone.com

Steps to Follow

- ☐ Study the vocabulary of **Presentación de vocabulario** (pp. 278–279) by looking at the photos and reading the words and accompanying text. Watch the DVD and complete the Video Activities Copymasters.
- ☐ Practice the words of the **Más vocabulario** box on page 278. Read the words aloud. Write the words in your notebook.
- ☐ Do **Práctica de vocabulario** (p. 280). Complete **Actividades 1**, **2**, and **3**.
- ☐ Complete *Cuaderno,* pages 220, 221, and 222.
  OR
  Complete *Cuaderno para hispanohablantes,* pages 220, 221, 222, and 223.
- ☐ Check your comprehension by completing the **Para y piensa** box on page 280.
- ☐ Complete the Did You Get It? Copymasters, pages 12 and 13.

If You Don't Understand...

- ☐ Use the images to help you understand the DVD.
- ☐ Listen to the CD in a quiet place. If you get lost, stop the CD and go back.
- ☐ Do the activities you understand first.
- ☐ Read the model before starting so you know what to do. Follow the model.
- ☐ Write down any questions you have for your teacher.
- ☐ If the activity has parts for two people, practice both parts.
- ☐ After you write a sentence, check to make sure that it says what you wanted to say.
- ☐ Use the Interactive Flashcards to help you study the lesson.

Absent Student Copymasters

Level 2 pp. 281–282

Vocabulario en contexto

Materials Checklist

- ☐ Student text
- ☐ DVD 2
- ☐ Video Activities Copymasters, pages 59 and 60
- ☐ TXT CD 6 Track 13
- ☐ Did You Get It? Copymasters, pages 12, 14, and 21

Steps to Follow

- ☐ Look at the photo on page 281. What do you think is happening?
- ☐ Read **Cuando lees** and **Cuando escuchas** under *Strategies* (p. 281). Copy the questions.
- ☐ Try to answer the questions in **Cuando lees** before watching the DVD.
- ☐ Watch DVD 2 without your book. Then watch the video again and complete the Video Activities Copymasters.
- ☐ Look at the dialogue in the book. Follow along in the book as you watch and listen to the DVD. Use the pictures and context to help you understand the dialogue.
- ☐ Complete **Actividades 4** and **5** on page 282.
- ☐ Check your comprehension by completing the **Para y piensa** box on page 282.
- ☐ Complete the Did You Get It? Copymasters, pages 12, 14, and 21.

If You Don't Understand...

- ☐ Watch the DVD in a quiet place. If you get lost, stop and replay the segment.
- ☐ Listen to the CD as many times as necessary.
- ☐ Read the activity directions again. Write the directions in your own words.
- ☐ Write the model on your paper. Try to follow the model in your own answers.
- ☐ Read aloud everything that you write. Be sure that you understand what you are reading.
- ☐ Write down any questions you have for your teacher.
- ☐ Practice both parts of any partner activities.
- ☐ Think about what you are trying to say when you write a sentence. After you write your sentence, check to make sure that it says what you wanted to say.

Absent Student Copymasters

Level 2 pp. 283–285

Presentación / Práctica de gramática

Materials Checklist

- ☐ Student text
- ☐ *Cuaderno,* pages 223–225
- ☐ *Cuaderno para hispanohablantes,* pages 224–226
- ☐ TXT CD 6 Track 14
- ☐ Did You Get It? Copymasters, pages 15 and 16
- ☐ ClassZone.com

Steps to Follow

- ☐ Study affirmative and negative words (p. 283).
- ☐ Do **Actividades 6**, **7**, **8**, and **9** (pp. 284–285). Use TXT CD 6 Track 14 with **Actividad 7.**
- ☐ Complete *Cuaderno,* pages 223, 224, and 225.
  OR
  Complete *Cuaderno para hispanohablantes,* pages 224, 225, and 226.
- ☐ Check your comprehension by completing the **Para y piensa** box on page 285.
- ☐ Complete the Did You Get It? Copymasters, pages 15 and 16.

If You Don't Understand...

- ☐ For activities that require listening, listen to the CD in a quiet place. If you get lost, stop the CD and go back.
- ☐ Do the activities you understand first.
- ☐ Reread the activity directions. Write the directions in your own words.
- ☐ Write the model on your paper. Try to follow the model in your own answers.
- ☐ Write down any questions you have for your teacher.
- ☐ Practice both parts of any partner activities.
- ☐ Read your answers aloud to make sure they say what you wanted to say.
- ☐ Use the Animated Grammar to help you understand.
- ☐ Use the Leveled Grammar Practice on the @Home Tutor.

Absent Student Copymasters

Level 2 pp. 286–287

Gramática en contexto

Materials Checklist

- ☐ Student Text
- ☐ DVD 2
- ☐ Video Activities Copymasters, pages 61 and 62
- ☐ TXT CD 6 Track 15
- ☐ Did You Get It? Copymasters, pages 15 and 17

Steps to Follow

- ☐ Look at the photo on page 286. What do you think is happening?
- ☐ Read **Cuando lees** and **Cuando escuchas** under *Strategies* (p. 286). Copy the questions.
- ☐ Read the script and try to understand the dialogue based on the picture. Try to answer the question in **Cuando lees.**
- ☐ Watch DVD 2 without your book. Then watch the DVD again and complete the Video Activities Copymasters.
- ☐ Look at the dialogue in the book. Follow along in the book as you watch and listen to the DVD. Use the pictures and context to help you understand the dialogue.
- ☐ Study the words in the **También se dice** box.
- ☐ Complete **Actividades 10**, **11**, and **12** on page 287.
- ☐ Check your comprehension by completing the **Para y piensa** box on page 287.
- ☐ Complete the Did You Get It? Copymasters, pages 15 and 17.

If You Don't Understand...

- ☐ Make sure you are in an area where you can concentrate.
- ☐ Review the section before completing the activities.
- ☐ Read the model a few times so you are certain that you understand what to do. Follow the model.
- ☐ Read everything aloud. Be sure that you understand what you are reading.
- ☐ Write down any questions you have for your teacher.
- ☐ If the activity has parts for two people, do both parts of the activity.
- ☐ Think about what you are trying to say when you write a sentence. After you write your sentence, check to make sure that it says what you wanted to say.

Absent Student Copymasters

Level 2 **pp. 288–290**

Presentación / Práctica de gramática

Materials Checklist

- ☐ Student text
- ☐ *Cuaderno,* pages 226–228
- ☐ *Cuaderno para hispanohablantes,* pages 227–230
- ☐ TXT CD 6 Tracks 16–17
- ☐ Did You Get It? Copymasters, pages 18 and 19
- ☐ ClassZone.com

Steps to Follow

- ☐ Study double object pronouns (p. 288).
- ☐ Do **Actividades 13** and **14** (p. 289).
- ☐ Listen to the **Pronunciación** section of TXT CD 6 Track 16. Pronounce the words aloud.
- ☐ Do **Actividad 15** (p. 290). Listen to TXT CD 6 Track 17 to complete the activity.
- ☐ Complete *Cuaderno,* pages 226, 227, and 228.
  OR
  Complete *Cuaderno para hispanohablantes,* pages 227, 228, 229, and 230.
- ☐ Check your comprehension by completing the **Para y piensa** box on page 290.
- ☐ Complete the Did You Get It? Copymasters, pages 18 and 19.

If You Don't Understand…

- ☐ For activities that require listening, listen to the CD in a quiet place. If you get lost, stop the CD and go back.
- ☐ Review the activity directions and study the model, if there is one. Try to follow the model in your own answers.
- ☐ Say what you want to write before you write it.
- ☐ If you have any questions, write them down for your teacher.
- ☐ Read your answers aloud to make sure they say what you wanted to say.
- ☐ Use the Animated Grammar to help you understand.
- ☐ Use the Leveled Grammar Practice on the @Home Tutor.

Absent Student Copymasters

Level 2 pp. 291–293

Todo junto

Materials Checklist

- ☐ Student text
- ☐ DVD 2
- ☐ Video Activities Copymasters, pages 63 and 64
- ☐ *Cuaderno,* pages 229–230
- ☐ *Cuaderno para hispanohablantes,* pages 231–232
- ☐ TXT CD 6 Tracks 11–14
- ☐ Did You Get It? Copymasters, pages 18 and 20
- ☐ WB CD 3 Tracks 11–14
- ☐ HL CD 2 Tracks 5–8

Steps to Follow

- ☐ Look at the photos on page 291. What do you think is happening?
- ☐ Read **Cuando lees** and **Cuando escuchas** under *Strategies* (p. 291). Copy the questions.
- ☐ Review the content of DVD 2.
- ☐ Read the script and try to understand the dialogue based on the picture. Try to answer the questions in **Cuando lees.**
- ☐ Watch DVD 2 without your book. Then watch the DVD again and complete the Video Activities Copymasters.
- ☐ Look at the dialogue in the book. Follow along as you watch and listen to the DVD. Use the pictures and context to help you understand the dialogue.
- ☐ Complete **Actividades 17**, **18**, **19**, **20**, and **21** on pages 292–293. Listen to TXT CD 6 Tracks 19–20 with **Actividad 20.**
- ☐ Complete *Cuaderno,* pages 229 and 230.
  OR
  Complete *Cuaderno para hispanohablantes,* pages 231 and 232.
- ☐ Check your comprehension by completing the **Para y piensa** box on page 293.
- ☐ Complete the Did You Get It? Copymasters, pages 18 and 20.

Absent Student Copymasters

Level 2 **pp. 294–295**

Lectura cultural

Materials Checklist

- ☐ Student text
- ☐ TXT CD 6 Track 21

Steps to Follow

- ☐ Read *Strategy:* **Leer** (p. 294).
- ☐ Read **Dos tradiciones culinarias** on pages 294 and 295.
- ☐ Look at the photos and reread the text.
- ☐ Follow along with the text on TXT CD 6 Track 21.
- ☐ Check your comprehension by completing the **¿Comprendiste?** and **¿Y tú?** sections of **Para y piensa** box on page 295.

If You Don't Understand...

- ☐ Make sure you are in an area where you can concentrate.
- ☐ Listen to the CD as many times as necessary.
- ☐ Read everything aloud. Be sure that you understand what you are reading.
- ☐ Write down any questions you have for your teacher.
- ☐ Think about what you are trying to say when you write a sentence. After you write your sentence, check to make sure that it says what you wanted to say.

Nombre ______________________ Clase ______________ Fecha ______________

Absent Student Copymasters

Level 2 p. 296

Proyectos culturales

Materials Checklist

- ☐ Student text
- ☐ Toasted bread
- ☐ Olive oil
- ☐ Ham
- ☐ Garlic
- ☐ Tomatoes

Steps to Follow

- ☐ Read **Comparación cultural** and the recipe in **Proyecto 2** (p. 296).
- ☐ Make Spanish tapas by following the recipe in **Proyecto 1**.
- ☐ Complete **En tu comunidad**.

If You Don't Understand...

- ☐ Read the activity directions again. Write out the directions in your own words.
- ☐ Use the photos as a guide.
- ☐ If you have any questions, write them down so you can ask your teacher later.

Nombre ________________ Clase ________________ Fecha ________________

Absent Student Copymasters

Level 2 pp. 298–299

Repaso de la lección

Materials Checklist

- ☐ Student text
- ☐ *Cuaderno,* pages 231–242
- ☐ *Cuaderno para hispanohablantes,* pages 233–242
- ☐ TXT CD 6 Track 22
- ☐ WB CD 3 Tracks 15–20

Steps to Follow

- ☐ Read the bullet points under **¡Llegada!** on page 298.
- ☐ Complete **Actividades 1**, **2**, **3**, **4**, and **5** (pp. 298–299). Listen to TXT CD 6 Track 22 to complete **Actividad 1**.
- ☐ Complete *Cuaderno,* pages 231, 232, and 233.
- ☐ Complete *Cuaderno,* pages 234, 235, and 236.
  OR
  Complete *Cuaderno para hispanohablantes,* pages 233, 234, and 235–236.
- ☐ Complete *Cuaderno,* pages 237, 238, and 239.
  OR
  Complete *Cuaderno para hispanohablantes,* pages 237, 238, and 239.
- ☐ Complete *Cuaderno,* pages 240, 241, and 242.
  OR
  Complete *Cuaderno para hispanohablantes,* pages 240, 241, and 242.

If You Don't Understand...

- ☐ Listen to the CD as many times as you need to complete the activity.
- ☐ Read the activity directions again. Write the directions in your own words.
- ☐ Write the model on your paper. Try to follow the model in your own answers.
- ☐ Say what you want to write before you write it.
- ☐ If you have any questions, write them down for your teacher to answer later.

Absent Student Copymasters

Level 2 pp. 300–301

Comparación cultural

Materials Checklist

- ☐ Student text
- ☐ *Cuaderno,* pages 243–245
- ☐ *Cuaderno para hispanohablantes,* pages 243–245
- ☐ TXT CD 6 Track 23

Steps to Follow

- ☐ Read the directions in **Lectura y escritura** for **Actividades 1** and **2** on page 300.
- ☐ Listen to TXT CD 6 Track 23 as you read **¡Qué delicioso!** in the text (pp. 300–301).
- ☐ Read the *Strategy:* **Escribir**, then begin **Actividad 2**.
- ☐ Complete the **Compara con tu mundo** section on page 300.
- ☐ Complete *Cuaderno,* pages 243, 244, and 245.
  OR
  Complete *Cuaderno para hispanohablantes,* pages 243, 244, and 245.

If You Don't Understand...

- ☐ Look over all the instructions for **Leer** and **Escribir** before you begin to read the feature.
- ☐ Listen to the CD in a quiet place. Pause and go back as often as necessary. Repeat unfamiliar words aloud.
- ☐ Look up words you don't know. Keep a list of new vocabulary.
- ☐ If you get confused, make a list of questions to ask your teacher later.
- ☐ Think about what you want to say before you begin writing. Reread everything you write. Check for punctuation, spelling and verb-subject agreement.

Absent Student Copymasters

Repaso inclusivo

Materials Checklist

- ☐ Student text
- ☐ TXT CD 6 Track 24

Steps to Follow

- ☐ Listen to TXT CD 6 Track 24 to do **Actividad 1** on page 304. Answer the questions with complete sentences.
- ☐ Complete **Actividades 2, 3, 4, 5, 6,** and **7** (pp. 304–305).
- ☐ Host your own cooking show for **Actividad 2** on page 304. Record your show on audio or video, if you can. If not, write out your script.
- ☐ Write a restaurant guide for **Actividad 5** on page 305.
- ☐ Take a survey for **Actividad 7** on page 305.

If You Don't Understand...

- ☐ Do the activities you understand first.
- ☐ Listen to the CD as many times as you need to complete **Actividad 1**.
- ☐ Read the activity directions again. Write the directions in your own words.
- ☐ Say what you want to write before you write it.
- ☐ Write down any questions you have for your teacher.
- ☐ Practice both parts of any partner activities.
- ☐ After you write a sentence, check to make sure that it says what you wanted to say.